YOU CAN'T ORDER CHANGE

YOU CAN'T
ORDER CHANGE

LESSONS FROM JIM McNERNEY'S
TURNAROUND AT BOEING

Peter S. Cohan

PORTFOLIO

PORTFOLIO
Published by the Penguin Group
Penguin Group (USA) Inc., 375 Hudson Street, New York, New York 10014, U.S.A. •
Penguin Group (Canada), 90 Eglinton Avenue East, Suite 700, Toronto, Ontario, Canada
M4P 2Y3 (a division of Pearson Penguin Canada Inc.) • Penguin Books Ltd, 80 Strand,
London WC2R 0RL, England • Penguin Ireland, 25 St. Stephen's Green, Dublin 2, Ire-
land (a division of Penguin Books Ltd.) • Penguin Books Australia Ltd, 250 Camberwell
Road, Camberwell, Victoria 3124, Australia (a division of Pearson Australia Group Pty Ltd)
• Penguin Books India Pvt. Ltd, 11 Community Centre, Panchsheel Park, New Delhi—110
017, India • Penguin Group (NZ), 67 Apollo Drive, Rosedale, North Shore 0632, New Zealand (a division of Pearson New Zealand Ltd) • Penguin Books (South Africa) (Pty) Ltd,
24 Sturdee Avenue, Rosebank, Johannesburg 2196, South Africa

Penguin Books Ltd, Registered Offices:
80 Strand, London WC2R 0RL, England

First published in 2008 by Portfolio,
a member of Penguin Group (USA) Inc.

1   3   5   7   9   10   8   6   4   2

Copyright © Peter S. Cohan, 2008
All rights reserved

While the author has made every effort to provide accurate telephone numbers and Internet addresses at the time of publication, neither the publisher nor the author assumes any
responsibility for errors, or for changes that occur after publication. Further, publisher does
not have any control over and does not assume any responsibility for author or third-party
Web sites or their content.

LIBRARY OF CONGRESS CATALOGING IN PUBLICATION DATA

Cohan, Peter S., 1957–
You can't order change : lessons from Jim McNerney's turnaround at Boeing Peter S.
Cohan.
p.   cm.
Includes bibliographical references and index.
ISBN 978-1-59184-239-2
1. Boeing Company—Management.   2. McNerny, W. James, 1949–
3. Leadership—United States.   4. Corporate culture—United States.   5. Aircraft
industry—United States—Management—Case studies.   I. Title.   II. Title: Jim
McNerney's turnaround at Boeing.
HD9711.U64B6434 2009
658.4—dc22   2008029793

Printed in the United States of America
Set in Aldus
Designed by Daniel Lagin

To Chuck Roush,
an inspiring leader and lifetime mentor

CONTENTS

YOU CAN'T ORDER CHANGE

INTRODUCTION

YOU CAN'T ORDER CHANGE

This is a book about the leadership style and practices of Jim McNerney. The current CEO of Boeing Co. spent much of his career as a rising star and major player at General Electric, where he was one of the three finalists to replace Jack Welch. When Welch gave that job to Jeff Immelt in 2000, 3M's board recruited McNerney, and he quickly set about revitalizing the tired old industrial giant. Now at Boeing, he has cleaned up a mass of legal problems, tackled the cultural issues that allowed them to arise, rebuilt the brand, and invested in new programs that promise a long, profitable future for the company.

A talented leader, McNerney worked with and learned from one of the greatest—GE's Jack Welch. He knows the importance of getting results, but he also knows that the way he gets those results is just as important. McNerney is a very smart leader: He's smart about motivating people; crafting business strategies that spark profitable growth; making operations more efficient and effective; and creating harmony within communities.

But McNerney approached the change process in a very respectful way. For example, when he joined 3M, McNerney set what was then an ambitious goal of increasing sales and operating earnings by at least 10 percent each year, nearly twice the rate of the past decade. He clearly saw these goals as within the reach of 3M's employees, but he chose not to order 3M to achieve these goals. Instead, he tried to "win the hearts and minds of employees." As McNerney said, "You can't order change. After all, there's only one of me and 75,000 of them."

The financial results he has generated are impressive. But this is not a book about numbers. It's a book about a leadership style that is very different and yet powerfully effective. As a McKinsey consultant prior to beginning his career at GE, McNerney honed his ability to diagnose business problems and work with others—both within McKinsey and at the client organizations—to achieve solutions. He understands that intellectual and emotional capital are critical assets. After all, subtract the brainpower and intellectual property that its people create, there's not much to a consulting firm. And at each of the companies that he's led, McNerney has managed its people as the key source of new product ideas that boost the top line *and* the essential ingredient for making operations more efficient. He does that not by frightening them into performing but by tapping into their innate desire to improve and removing barriers that inhibit their growth.

As McNerney observed when he took over at 3M, the need to both boost revenues and cut costs is a unique imperative of the particular economic environment in which many companies currently operate. While in the past, companies went through times when boosting revenue alone or just cutting costs was enough for executives to achieve results, the world has changed. Thanks to globalization, information technology, and deregulation, companies can no longer afford to focus on just boosting revenues or cutting costs. They need to do both simultaneously. And in order to do that, leaders need to change how organizations operate at a fundamental level. McNerney knows this, but he has the intellectual humility to realize that he can't make these changes himself—to paraphrase, there's only one of him and tens of thousands of them, the employees.

McNERNEY'S TRACK RECORD

While this book is about leadership and not about the numbers, the numbers confirm the success of the leadership. Here are McNerney's.

TABLE ONE. 3M AND BOEING SELECTED FINANCIAL DATA FOR JIM MCNERNEY'S CEO TENURE

	3M	Boeing
Tenure as CEO	January 1, 2001–June 30, 2005	July 1, 2005–present*
Sales change	$16.1B to $21.2B	$54.8B to $67.0B
Annual sales growth rate	7 percent	7 percent
Profit change	$1.47B to $3.3B	$2.5B to $4.8B
Annual profit growth rate	22 percent	24 percent
Operating margin change	14.1 percent to 23.7 percent	5.1 percent to 9.4 percent
Stock price change	$55.33 to $72.30	$64.68 to $73.95
Stock price percent change	32 percent	14 percent
S&P 500 percent change	-12.8 percent	14 percent

Source: Morningstar, author analysis.
*Data as of June 9, 2008. Boeing 2008 sales and profit figures for the trailing twelve-month period.

HOW McNERNEY TACKLES ELEVEN LEADERSHIP CHALLENGES

Thanks to his broad general management experience, Jim McNerney has developed and tested his management techniques in many industries facing a range of challenges. In this book we are going to look at eleven leadership challenges and how McNerney overcomes them:

- **How does a leader unlock *individual* achievement?** McNerney sets a goal of making each individual 15 percent better. Rather than hog all the attention, he develops leaders. He works with people to define the behaviors he expects in a leader. He opens the flow of communication up and down the line and removes barriers that inhibit cooperation. He removes people who inhibit the development of others to boost their own careers. McNerney's goal is to build a deep bench of leaders.

- **How can a leader spur *groups to work together* for the greater corporate good?** Many organizations foster competition among different groups for scarce resources such as capital and higher position on the corporate ladder. McNerney works with groups to find goals that spur them to cooperate rather than compete. He picks strategies to achieve these common goals and removes obstacles that keep groups from cooperating to implement the strategies.

- **How can a company pay its leaders to boost long-term value rather than short-term stock price?** While paying leaders to spike stock price is a fad, McNerney pays leaders to reach financial goals that will increase the long-term value of the company. He does this by linking leaders' pay to the generating of profits that exceed the cost of capital needed to produce them. This has two benefits: It focuses people on factors they can control, and it removes any incentive to manipulate investment spending to meet short-term profit targets.

- **How do you develop technology to meet the needs of consumers?** McNerney achieves growth by building products that customers want to buy. Rather than encourage technologists to work by themselves to invent the new products that interest them, he makes engineers part of a team of different business functions that works with customers. McNerney challenges the team to build products that will satisfy the unmet needs of those customers. He kills development projects with weaker profit potential and uses the freed-up funds to ensure that the most promising projects can succeed.

- **How can a leader invest in strategies that beat the competition?** To beat the competition, McNerney funds bet-the-company strategies that satisfy three tests: They go after big, growing markets; they build on the company's strengths; and they take advantage of competitor weaknesses. If McNerney believes that those three tests can be satisfied, he places the bet because he thinks the company can win enough of that market's profits to earn an attractive return on the investment.

- **How much should a leader depend on acquisitions for growth?** McNerney does not depend on acquisitions for growth. He wants a company to grow based on the skills of its people. He views acquisitions in unrelated industries as highly risky because they tend to be expensive and hard to operate and integrate. However, if a business is already successful and an acquisition can help advance it without paying too much money, he will do it. McNerney's philosophy is that the more that growth comes from internal sources the better.

- **How can a newly appointed leader get quick results?** McNerney is a networker. He takes time to build networks with leaders inside and outside his organization. Sometimes these older networks can provide insights into a new organization, even before he arrives. But whether or not he arrives knowing anyone, he is quick to start talking and listening. McNerney quickly sizes up his new direct reports to figure out whom he can rely on to fix problems and seize opportunities. He learns which performance indicators affect financial results, and he analyzes these to pinpoint the highest-priority problems. Then he empowers his people to solve them. He rewards those who boost results through the right process. He helps those who struggle but can adapt, and he moves out those who can't.

- **How can a leader boost productivity?** McNerney believes in operating efficiently. At GE he used formal management methods to boost productivity in diverse operations. In the companies he leads, McNerney uses techniques such as Six Sigma—a formal method for improving operations—and Lean Manufacturing (or just "Lean")—a systematic approach to minimizing waste in manufacturing operations. However, he does not impose these techniques just because he has worked with them in the past. Instead, he gauges the organization to figure out which of the tools—if any—fit with the company's culture and his goals. Once he picks a management method, McNerney introduces it to the organization by training people. He helps choose specific improvement projects, gives teams the resources they need to succeed, removes obstacles, and rewards those who deliver.

- **How can a leader manage global product development?** McNerney approved and led a global network of suppliers to develop a breakthrough product—the Boeing 787 Dreamliner, a midsize, twin-engine jetliner that will carry between 210 and 330 passengers.[1] Boeing started the project before McNerney became CEO, but as a Boeing director and later as CEO, he has pushed its implementation. McNerney understands that Boeing has strengths and weaknesses and believes that it is smarter to outsource the things that others can do better. He has led Boeing to work with the world's best suppliers, to reduce its capital costs, and to shorten its time to market. This has required building productive relationships with suppliers around the world.

- **How can a leader create a culture of ethics and compliance?** McNerney took over Boeing at a time when it had struggled through years of costly ethical problems. He took short- and long-term action to create a culture that values ethics and compliance. He settled a lawsuit with the government. He added ethics to Boeing's values and expects leaders to set an example of ethical behavior. He encourages open discussion of ethical matters at all levels and has linked pay and promotion to ethical conduct. Finally, McNerney created a powerful legal and compliance unit to seek out ethical problems early.
- **How can a leader reduce a company's environmental impact?** McNerney takes responsibility for Boeing's environmental impact. He does this because he knows that he can create economic and social benefits for Boeing's communities by designing, building, and operating aircraft in a way that cuts the amount of noise and carbon that the aircraft produce. By reducing Boeing's environmental footprint, McNerney is winning new orders from airlines that value its product's reduced carbon emissions. And if that makes Boeing's communities better off in the bargain, McNerney is even happier.

WHO IS JIM McNERNEY?

If you face these challenges in your business and you're curious to learn more about how McNerney overcomes them, here's an introduction to your guide. Jim McNerney is a leader who gets results by motivating others. According to Boeing lead director

Kenneth Duberstein, who once served as President Ronald Reagan's chief of staff and recruited McNerney, "We wanted a change agent, someone who could communicate a commitment to ethics. Jim is the whole package: strong leader, visionary, motivator, team builder. He's very comfortable in his own skin."[2]

Was McNerney the right person for the job? Morgan Stanley analyst Heidi Wood was skeptical when he took over. She thought that Boeing was on the right trajectory, and her message to McNerney was "Don't fuck it up!" In her view, McNerney "had a fabulous pedigree." Her inquiries revealed that he had done a great job at GE Aircraft. However, she heard some pointless sniping from GE insiders that "McNerney was only going to Boeing so he could go into politics." And she heard mixed reviews of his tenure at 3M: Some thought his performance was "decent," others said "the jury's still out," and still others thought he was "terrible." Her conversations with McNerney revealed that he thought that "he did not do well on M&A [mergers and acquisitions]." And when she first met McNerney, she was determined not to be taken in by his "charm offensive" and his "pretty-boy résumé." However, she now believes that McNerney is "unique in Boeing's history and exactly what Boeing needs."[3]

As we'll see throughout this book, what makes McNerney the right leader at the right time for Boeing is his understanding that its future rests on making the right investments. These investments are bets on new products that he anticipates will meet the needs of its customers more effectively than do competitors'. And, as Wood suggests, decisions about people are a critical leading indicator of whether those investments will pay off for shareholders. How so? Because Boeing's bets can only succeed if the right people with the right skills manage those bets. Some bets need people who excel at creating a compelling vision for the future of the aircraft industry; other bets need people with a talent for managing aircraft manufacturing. And in Wood's view, McNerney's ability to develop Boeing's talent and to match people and projects is seeding Boeing's future with a string of profitable bets that will pay off for Boeing shareholders.[4]

So what is the source of McNerney's ability? McNerney embodies a core midwestern value writ large—don't break your arm patting yourself on the back. This is an expression first articulated to me a few years ago by John Bachmann, the former managing director of Edward Jones, a St. Louis, Missouri–based brokerage firm, which hires for its offices entrepreneurs who build credibility in communities by achieving steady results for clients.[5]

It's not that McNerney is not competitive and doesn't like to win. It's just that he prefers to let the organization's results speak for themselves rather than drawing all the attention to himself.

McNerney has punched all the right cards throughout his life. The son of a Chicago health care executive, McNerney achieved academically and athletically. He attended Yale University, where he played on its baseball team, and Harvard Business School. Moreover, McNerney has excelled at such prestigious companies as Procter & Gamble, McKinsey & Co., and GE, where he outperformed his peers for nineteen years until he lost out in the succession battle for Welch's job.

McNerney didn't lose out to Jeff Immelt because of his performance. During his four-year tenure at GE Aircraft Engines, McNerney increased revenue from $7.8 billion to $10.8 billion, making it GE's single biggest source of profit. The reason McNerney lost is a different statistic—age. Welch wanted to replace himself with someone who would have the same twenty-year tenure that he had enjoyed. Immelt was forty-four at the time, while McNerney was fifty-one.[6]

But in the mind of this GE shareholder, Welch might have chosen the wrong man. Under Immelt, GE stock is 24 percent below where it was when he took over from Welch in September

2001, while the S&P 500 is up 21 percent. By contrast, between January 2001 and June 2005 under McNerney, 3M stock rose 32 percent. And since July 1, 2005, when he took over as CEO, and June 9, 2008, Boeing's stock rose 14 percent.[7]

"YOU CAN'T ORDER CHANGE" ROAD MAP

To illustrate how McNerney succeeds, I've organized the leadership challenges and the way he overcomes them into eleven management imperatives. As depicted in Figure 1 below, *You Can't Order Change* covers these in separate chapters organized around four broad categories: leadership, strategy, operations, and communities.

Figure 1. The McNerney Way

Place Leadership Development at the Top of Your Priority List.
McNerney recognizes that he can't do everything himself and
that for Boeing to succeed, it must develop strong bench strength.
It needs new leaders who can tackle the challenges required of a
growing company in a competitive industry. The following three
chapters present McNerney's approach to developing leaders:

- **Chapter 1. Help Your People Get 15 Percent Better.** McNerney motivates people to get 15 percent better every year—and
  in so doing, boosts financial performance. Specifically, he focuses on people who have the potential to change due to their
  openness, courage, and teamwork. And he views his job as
  removing the bureaucratic obstacles that keep them from "ig-
  niting." To get there he encourages the flow of information up
  and down the line. He gets *phenomenally talented assholes*
  out of the line, and he invests in leadership development.[8]
- **Chapter 2. Lead Groups to Higher Ground.** McNerney finds
  common aims for groups both inside and outside the company that have traditionally competed with each other. For
  example, he can take a team of people from different functions and urge them to debate the issues openly. He pushes
  them to develop a strategy to which they all agree. And that
  sense of shared ownership spurs better results.
- **Chapter 3. Link Pay to Profit and Process, Not Stock Price.**
  McNerney has instituted a subtle but important shift in the
  way managers at Boeing are paid. He recognizes that managers can't control Boeing's stock price so he has increased the
  proportion of their bonuses linked to what managers can
  control—their organization's profit. His notion is that the
  best business leaders make efficient use of the company's
  capital. For example, it's better for a business unit to earn
  $100 million of profit using $10 million of capital than to

generate that same $100 million in profit—but require $50 million of capital to get there. By measuring leaders on efficient use of capital, rather than boosting stock price, McNerney gets them to take responsibility for factors they can control; he eliminates their chance to make excuses for not performing; and he encourages them to pursue strategies that produce long-term value.

Pursue Strategies That Spark Organic Growth. McNerney believes that internally generated, organic growth is better than growing through acquisitions. The following chapters describe how McNerney develops such organic growth strategies:

- **Chapter 4. Build Strategy on Customer Focus.** Through his own example, McNerney gets engineers to understand the customer. By listening to passengers' fear of confinement and complaints about the discomfort of jet lag and by understanding airlines' changing route strategies, McNerney encouraged Boeing's product development teams to use composite technology as part of a design that would make customers happier. McNerney manages innovation so it yields products whose benefits make customers eager to buy.

- **Chapter 5. Invest in Your Strengths.** When McNerney was a director of Boeing in 2003, two years before signing on as CEO, he approved what ultimately amounted to a $10 billion investment in a new aircraft—the 787. The investment bolstered Boeing's ability to win a big share of a three-thousand-aircraft midrange market segment. It built on Boeing's strengths in design, systems integration, and support. And it took advantage of competitor Airbus's internal rivalries to garner a five-year time-to-market lead with a technologically superior aircraft.

- **Chapter 6. Grow Through People, Not Deals.** McNerney believes that organic growth—which stems from a company's existing products and people—is more profitable than growth through acquisitions of unrelated businesses. He encourages organic growth by selling products developed domestically into international markets; by changing an organization's structure from a product to a customer focus; and by encouraging different business units to cooperate so they can gain share in developing markets. McNerney does not shun all acquisitions, though. He does deals that add to already successful business lines.

Tighten Operations to Reduce Costs and Increase Productivity. In a company of Boeing's size and history, McNerney sees many opportunities to increase productivity. Boeing benefits in this quest for greater efficiency from McNerney's prior experience, as he applies powerful management methods, such as Six Sigma and Lean, perfected at GE and other companies. The following chapters detail McNerney's approach to productivity improvement:

- **Chapter 7. Tackle Challenging Situations Quickly and Effectively.** McNerney filters hundreds of problems and opportunities down to the critical few within a period of months after taking on a new position. For instance, at GE Aircraft Engines he quickly figured out that his business plan would be at risk unless his team could figure out a way to stop competitors from making lower-priced versions of its profitable spare engine parts. He assembled a team of patent attorneys, engineers, and manufacturing experts to develop and build a more advanced, patent-protected line of spare parts that would be tough for competitors to knock off. McNerney boosts the careers of people who support these solutions to high-priority problems—and lets those who can't adapt go.
- **Chapter 8. Tighten Operations with Process-Improvement Tools.** When McNerney wanted to improve productivity at

3M and Boeing, he used distinct methods at each. He boosted 3M's margins from 17 percent in 2001 to 23 percent in 2005 with help from Six Sigma. And at Boeing he used Lean to cut in half the time it takes to assemble a 737—from twenty-two days to eleven days, to save hundreds of millions of dollars, and to increase capacity without adding new plant.[9]

- **Chapter 9. Partner with Global Suppliers to Reduce Risk and Accelerate Time to Market.** McNerney oversaw the outsourcing of a record 70 percent of work on the 787 to more than fifty suppliers working twenty-four hours a day at 135 sites on four continents designing and building 787 parts.[10] McNerney trusted the original 787 general manager and vice president, Mike Bair, to manage this process; however, after a series of unpleasant surprises, such as the fact that the first 787 arrived at Boeing with missing systems and 1,000 temporary fasteners in the wing and fuselage, McNerney replaced him with Pat Shanahan, until then a vice president in Boeing's Missile Defense unit, known as a "hard-ass" manager. By pushing Boeing to meet with its suppliers and their subcontractors, McNerney has changed the way it manages these partnerships. McNerney now spends enough time with people on the line that he knows when leaders are sharing problems with him and when they're not.

Establish More Harmonious Relationships with Communities. McNerney has strengthened Boeing's relationships with the communities in which it operates. To that end, he has taken steps to encourage ethics and integrity. The following chapters explore McNerney's approach to harmonizing Boeing's relationships with its communities:

- **Chapter 10. Make Ethics and Compliance a Clear Competitive Advantage.** McNerney took over Boeing at a time when its many ethical problems had cost it a huge air force contract—as well as several top executives. He settled with the government, which had sued Boeing, and ended up paying a $615 million fine.[11] Through a change in Boeing's values, a reward system that boosts the careers of those who get results the right way, and a central organization charged with surfacing ethical problems early, McNerney has drained Boeing's ethical quagmire.

- **Chapter 11. Cut Your Company's Environmental Footprint.** McNerney believes strongly that Boeing needs to create products that produce less air and noise pollution. That's a priority for him because he thinks it's the right thing to do for Boeing's communities and because it helps Boeing win new orders. He cuts Boeing's environmental footprint by investing in new technologies that let its products consume less fuel, generate fewer pollutants, and make less noise as they fly. McNerney also works with regulators and others in the industry to set more stringent environmental standards. And he put a strong executive in charge of Boeing's Environmental Strategy department to embed his concern with cutting its environmental footprint deep into Boeing's culture.

I've learned much from observing Jim McNerney. You can too. Read on.

CHAPTER 1.

HELP YOUR PEOPLE GET 15 PERCENT BETTER

Boeing's CEO McNerney doesn't get too personally involved in the details of strategy. Instead, he focuses his attention on developing the people who run Boeing's businesses. Like all corporate leaders, he wants to accelerate the growth of quantitative measures of corporate success such as revenues, profits, and cash flow, but McNerney has set his goal as making Boeing's people 15 percent better every year. By this he means improving both the effectiveness of individuals and how all the people in the whole organization work together. The number may sound arbitrary, but McNerney uses it to let people know that he's measuring what they do.

Jim McNerney focuses on people's growth because he believes that if the company's *people* grow, then the company will grow. To encourage people to grow, McNerney sets goals that stretch people beyond their comfort zones, and he urges managers from the top down to be role models. He expects them to chart the course for employees, to inspire them to reach for performance, to exhibit the courage to do the right thing, and to bring the right values to the job.

McNerney sees himself as a value-adding facilitator rather than as a commander "crashing through the waves on the bridge of a frigate."[1] He thinks about how he can help others improve. He tries to figure out how to unlock the creativity that he feels is often trapped inside people in a stifling, bureaucratic environment. McNerney's emphasis on enhancing people's productivity is relevant for both individual contributors and those who manage them.

Throughout his career, McNerney has improved the financial and stock market performance of every organization he has led. He has accomplished that with his people-focused leadership approach. Specifically, McNerney does five things that help the people in his organizations perform more effectively:

- He defines clear leadership attributes
- He interacts with people so they jointly own the leadership attributes
- He encourages communication from bottom up
- He gets rid of players who block others
- He invests in developing leaders

HE DEFINES CLEAR LEADERSHIP ATTRIBUTES

McNerney starts by engaging people throughout the organization in a conversation about what leadership means. His objective is to reach a consensus around specific "leadership attributes." He uses these attributes to align individual performance goals with the organization's direction. The attributes provide a framework within which employees set goals and strive to achieve them. Once he and his people agree on the goals, McNerney can chart over time how well each person is achieving them.

He clearly did this during his first CEO role at 3M. Viewing leadership development as "one of the most important parts of my job as the leader," McNerney spent a year working with the organization to define leadership "in a 3M context." This global definition transcended 3M's products and the countries in which it operated. McNerney concluded that 3M leaders needed to be able to do six things extremely well:

- Chart a course for themselves and for the people who work for them
- Continually raise expectations in a reasonable way, or raise the bar every year
- Motivate and energize other people
- Innovate resourcefully
- Live 3M's ethical and compliance-oriented values
- Deliver results

By defining explicit leadership attributes in collaboration with the people in the organization, McNerney not only ensures that people really understand what each of the attributes means, but also gets them emotionally engaged in supporting the attributes. Defining clear leadership attributes further allows McNerney to link career development programs, as well as individuals' evaluations and compensation, to the attributes. For example, at 3M McNerney changed people-development systems, such as training both in the classroom and on the job, and he created leadership career paths and compensation programs, all with an eye toward fostering the leadership attributes. McNerney used the leadership attribute "lead inclusively" to encourage leaders to bring out, learn from, and act on knowledge from the bottom or outside the organization.[2]

The leadership attributes that framed McNerney's efforts to fix Boeing's culture were almost exactly the same as the ones at 3M:

- Chart the course
- Set high expectations

- Inspire others
- Find a way
- Live the Boeing values (the most important of which is un-swerving integrity)[3]
- Deliver results[4]

McNerney defines clear leadership attributes because he knows that what gets measured gets done. While the leadership attributes aren't surprising, they're valuable because they motivate and direct the behavior of people with leadership ambitions. The attributes he used at 3M and Boeing emphasize setting ever higher goals and motivating people to achieve them in a manner consistent with company values. McNerney promotes those whose behavior stands out as being most consistent with the leadership attributes. And he sidelines those who cling to the old ways.

HE INTERACTS WITH PEOPLE SO THEY JOINTLY OWN THE LEADERSHIP ATTRIBUTES

These attributes, while clearly defined above, would be of little value to the organization were McNerney simply to impose his own personal definition of leadership by edict. While his opinions carry significant weight, to get buy-in from the people in the organization, those people need to have input. McNerney believes that the leadership framework should emerge from the organization after many conversations among its people. At Boeing, simply holding the conversations helped McNerney steer the culture toward greater individual initiative and achievement after years of command-and-control leaders who expected people just to carry out orders.

When McNerney takes on a new leadership role, he holds a series of town meetings with employees in which, through give-

and-take conversations, he subtly sells his vision. He does this by listening to what employees like and dislike about the culture. And he inquires whether the leadership attributes that he hopes to promote might help improve the culture. Through such conversations, McNerney communicates his ideas about leadership and absorbs people's reactions to them. After a year of such conversations, people feel that they have created the list of leadership attributes. Once people "own" them, it becomes relatively straightforward to link their professional goals to them. And from there, McNerney and his managers can measure people's performance relative to the goals and provide appropriate incentives.

McNerney worked closely with the heads of Boeing's business units to agree on a set of leadership attributes, much as he had at 3M. In his view, the greatest threat to Boeing was that its success could "become the seed of arrogance and then failure."[5] To root out complacency, McNerney spent time discussing what had gone wrong in the past and spreading the awareness of need for change throughout Boeing.[6]

McNerney inherited a Boeing culture with a wide gap between his vision and what it could become. The leadership attributes became a sort of bridge between the past and the future. They included some traits of the old Boeing, such as the emphasis on high expectations and delivering results, but they also added new ideas, such as inspiring others and acting with integrity. In the command-and-control Boeing that McNerney inherited, inspiration was not necessary because people would do what their bosses told them to do. McNerney wanted Boeing's managers to take the time to inspire workers, rather than intimidating them based on rank.

McNerney's investment in ensuring that he and his people co-own the leadership attributes suggests three leadership lessons:

- Leadership attributes are the foundation of changing a company's culture.
- A CEO seeking to make fundamental changes must listen and broadcast over a long period of time to create a shared sense of ownership of the change.
- To change behavior, leaders must link the attributes to performance evaluation, pay, and promotion.

HE ENCOURAGES COMMUNICATION
FROM THE BOTTOM UP

During his nineteen years at GE, McNerney learned that only the bottom line mattered. He drove people to make quarterly improvements in financial performance. But, while leading people to improve performance depends heavily on setting goals and pushing people to achieve them, it also depends on learning enough about their particular areas to be able to understand their problems and work across the organization to generate workable solutions. McNerney is not an expert in aircraft technology; however, his ability to see how technical choices affect whether customers will buy Boeing's products reflects his great ability to learn from others.

Creating this dialogue in technical organizations like GE Aircraft and Boeing is a stretch for McNerney because he isn't an engineer.[7] However, McNerney impressed the engineers at GE Aircraft Engines because within two years, he could sit in a design meeting and ask intelligent questions about technical issues such as compression and temperature distribution. He learned enough about technology, and people appreciated his ability to learn and understand how engines are designed. This understanding allowed McNerney to go to an airline and talk to its executives about their business problems—such as yields and city pairs (the combination of departure and arrival airports). This same skill has been of great value to McNerney at Boeing.[8] By taking the time to learn the language of the design engineers, McNerney sent them a signal that he wanted to learn from them and use their ideas to make Boeing a more effective competitor.

McNerney has a knack for getting people below him in an organization to share information. His personality is even and outgoing. He puts people at ease and is not intimidating. When he stands in front of them, he uses humor to get the audience on his side. He does not drive fear into his people. He says, "Here is what we've got to do. How do we get the stagecoach to go faster?" He'll talk about baseball and hockey to set people at ease. And when things get difficult, he works through the problem with the employees. This is in stark contrast to Welch, who had a tendency to fire a guy when he made a bad mistake. McNerney works through the problem but lets the person know he saw the mistake.[9]

One of the reasons McNerney encourages the flow of information from the bottom up is so he can find talent. The information flow helps him distinguish between people who can grow 15 percent every year and those who can't. McNerney says that he has found that the people who grow most share specific personal characteristics, such as "openness to change, courage to change, hard work, [and] teamwork." McNerney believes that most people have these traits within them but that "a bureaucratic environment" often keeps them from blossoming. In McNerney's view, such environments constrain people, making them feel "beaten about the head and shoulders." He sees his job as changing the environment to unlock their natural ability to grow.[10]

McNerney tries to give opportunities to the people he sees as having the most potential to grow. He strives to make those people feel that they are directly "connected to the company's mission" instead of being a "cog in some manager's machine." In his experience, this connection happens—or as he puts it, "you get ignition"—when people become convinced that they are growing as they pursue company goals.[11]

McNerney also tries to encourage the flow of information up and down the line by adopting management processes that improve productivity. As we'll explore later, in chapter 8, McNerney achieved this when he introduced Six Sigma to 3M. This technique teaches people new ways to approach business problems and to lead other people. As Six Sigma helps managers achieve better results, they feel they're becoming better managers. And as this feeling of ignition spreads widely throughout an organization, McNerney believes that the company improves. He aligns the growth of people with the company's growth. This alignment unleashes people's motivation and enthusiasm, which helps boost corporate performance.[12]

At Boeing, McNerney wanted to encourage this same kind of alignment and enthusiasm. But before he could do that he needed to rid Boeing of the legacy of top-down-only information flow, which suppressed the people in what he considered to be a proud and capable culture. He started with the recognition that Boeing had a unique culture that elicited great pride in its people. The people who worked at Boeing had the same self-image as those who worked at companies like IBM and Microsoft; they saw themselves as industry leaders. This passion for the company made people very eager to work at Boeing and to spend their entire careers there. This led to a higher rate of management retention at Boeing than at many other companies. And despite the well-known up and down cycles of the airline industry, Boeing had an unusually high level of employee devotion.[13]

But earlier leaders had not harnessed that natural sense of pride in working for Boeing. They issued orders and promoted people who carried them out without question—creating an environment that was more responsive to internal cues than to external signals from customers and competitors. To tap into the passion and talent of Boeing's work force and encourage the flow of information from the bottom up, McNerney substituted the role of coach for the commanding leadership style of his predecessors. In particular, McNerney describes that coaching role as being a "value-added facilitator" whose values and courage to do the right thing will ultimately help others get better. McNerney also has a clear vision of what the CEO's job is not. He sees himself as the opposite of the hero who takes charge and imposes his will on an organization through force. McNerney gives people the power and intellectual latitude to seize opportunity rather than waiting for him to tell them what to do.

But McNerney's decision to empower people at Boeing was challenged as he tackled the difficulties of trying to meet the production schedule for the new 787. Many questioned whether there was sufficient flow of information from the bottom up or whether the manager of the 787 unit had bottled up that flow. After three delays in the 787's delivery schedule, in April 2008 McNerney intervened personally to change the top management of the program. This included moving aside the person in charge of the 787, Mike Bair, and replacing him with Pat Shanahan, until then a vice president in Boeing's Missile Defense unit.[14] McNerney also pushed executives to act more decisively, and he visited factory floors, sometimes speaking directly with assembly workers. Moreover, he received daily briefings on the 787's progress and ensured that Boeing managers become involved in suppliers' operations by stationing Boeing employees in every major supplier's factory. As McNerney said, "We've got 240 programs in the company, and there's one that's got more of my attention right now than any one, and that's the 787. Eventually, I hope we are defined by the 787. Just not right this instant."[15]

McNerney is, of course, intensely focused on the details of the

787 program because it is troubled. He is hoping to assure that it is ultimately seen as an only temporary blemish on Boeing's reputation. But it also reinforces the importance of encouraging the flow of information from the bottom up. If McNerney can continue to unfreeze these lines of communication, it will help him make Boeing 15 percent better.

McNerney's efforts to encourage the flow of information from the bottom up suggest four leadership lessons:

- Bureaucracies can create informal norms that stifle enthusiasm, creativity, and the flow of information up and down the line.
- A CEO needs to take action to strip away the vestiges of bureaucracy and unleash people's growth potential.
- One reason for the CEO to encourage the flow of information from the bottom up is to identify individuals with the potential to grow.
- CEOs must identify the right balance between empowering and trusting their leaders. One way to do this is by creating channels to tap into information from lower levels of the organization.

HE GETS RID OF PLAYERS WHO BLOCK OTHERS

Wall Street analysts who spend years covering a company learn the strengths and weaknesses of its top people. If the analysts believe that a company has done a good job of matching people to strategic initiatives, especially those with a big impact on earnings, such as meeting production schedules or long-term product development, they are likely to raise their earnings estimates. Conversely, if analysts conclude that a company is putting the wrong people in charge of critical projects, they will slash earnings forecasts. McNerney's decisions about who fills key slots thus send a powerful signal to Wall Street about whether Boeing's earnings goals will be achieved. So, by removing bad leaders and replacing them with better ones, McNerney knows he can boost Wall Street's confidence in Boeing's earnings prospects.

McNerney recognizes that his skill at managing Boeing's talent pool is critical to what actually happens inside Boeing as well as to the analysts' perceptions. McNerney does not pretend to be a visionary who can accurately predict the future of the aircraft industry and position Boeing accordingly. So he relies on having a smart, effective team in place. And this means that there is no room for people who sabotage subordinates in order to burnish their own reputations. In Wood's view, McNerney is a "more humanistic, thoughtful, intuitive, and sensitive leader than Phil Condit [who was Boeing's CEO from 1996 to 2003].[16] Condit could think 30 years ahead but he couldn't inspire the culture and did not pay much attention to ethics." McNerney, who isn't an aviation industry visionary, manages Boeing's talent pool. And, as Wood puts it, a critical aspect of managing that talent has been getting the "phenomenally talented assholes out of the center of power."[17]

This last concept requires some explanation. By *phenomenal* Wood means people who are brilliant in their area of expertise. At Boeing that could mean a range of important skills, such as being able to see far into the future of the industry or having a knack for designing an efficient aircraft manufacturing process. In her view, anyone near the top of Boeing is phenomenal in some way. Unfortunately, some of those who were prone to reaching the very top of the corporate ladder there were also *assholes*. By that she meant that these individuals would gladly throw any of their talented colleagues under the bus to advance their careers.[18]

In Wood's view, McNerney is quite skillful about moving those *phenomenal assholes* out of the center of power. This matters because if these *phenomenal assholes* win promotions, their promotions discourage all the *phenomenal team players* who have lost out on those opportunities. The result is that Boeing loses the talented people it needs as these discouraged workers seek employment elsewhere. So by subtly punishing people who push out their more team-oriented peers and rewarding people whose talents will encourage and motivate others, McNerney is building up Boeing's talent pool. Wood also believes that McNerney's management of Boeing's talent is critical to her ability to predict its earnings.

Earnings prospects help investors decide whether a company's stock is cheap or overpriced. For example, if a company's earnings growth is expected to outpace the ratio of its price to its earnings (P/E), then investors may conclude that the stock is cheap, whereas if the company's earnings growth is expected to drop below its P/E, then investors may conclude that the stock is expensive. For example, analysts calculate a ratio of the P/E to the forecasted earnings growth rate. If that P/E is 14 and the company's earnings are forecast to grow 28 percent, the analyst calculates a price/earnings–to–growth (PEG) ratio of 0.5 (14/28); in this case the analyst would consider the stock inexpensively priced because that PEG ratio is well below 1, at which the stock price is considered fair. If that PEG ratio were, say, 2 because the P/E of the stock was 56, the analyst would consider the stock to be expensive. Wall Street analysts who cover Boeing, such as Wood, forecast Boeing's earnings by trying to predict how much profit the sum of its current and new products will generate. The forecasts for current products contribute heavily to Boeing's earnings in the shorter term, whereas the forecasts for the new products help analysts decide the magnitude of Boeing's earnings further in the future as sales from its current products taper off.

Analysts who know Boeing well understand that getting the phenomenally talented assholes out of key jobs can make a big difference in whether Boeing makes its numbers. That's because these phenomenally talented assholes will try to inhibit the effectiveness of the phenomenally talented team players who just want to do a good job for the company. The assholes will do this because if the team players are operating effectively, they'll make the assholes look bad by comparison and cost them their coveted promotions.

How does this affect the way analysts forecast earnings? If a phenomenally talented team player runs a program, Wood puts a higher value on the company's earnings stream than if a phenomenally talented asshole is in charge. Based on her experience, she assumes that the phenomenally talented team player will motivate his or her people to work much harder—putting in a 120-hour workweek if needed—because they love their boss. As a result of that leader's motivational power, she will forecast that the program will generate 120 percent of the profit that the company predicts publicly. By contrast, if a phenomenally talented asshole is in charge, she will assume that the company will only achieve 80 percent of the predicted profit because people will only do the minimum needed to get the job done and might even do something subtle to make problems for their boss just out of spite.[19]

Wood believes that McNerney is one of the best when it comes to matching people to jobs. In her view, there are four tiers of executives:

1. Executives who can't distinguish between the sycophantic but phenomenally talented assholes and the phenomenally talented team players
2. Executives who can distinguish the two but don't care as long as the leaders make their numbers
3. Executives who put the phenomenally talented team players in positions of power and fire the phenomenally talented assholes

4. Executives who put the phenomenally talented team players in positions of power and keep the phenomenally talented assholes but move them out of their line positions while making them think that they are getting a promotion

Wood believes that McNerney is a tier 4 executive, the type who produces the best results for shareholders. He assigns phenomenally talented team players to manage people because they will get their people highly motivated to perform better. And Boeing will still have access to the knowledge and skills of the phenomenally talented assholes; they just won't be in positions to demotivate people working on important projects. If McNerney can put phenomenally talented team players in charge of its key projects, then analysts like Wood are likely to forecast higher earnings, which boosts Boeing's stock.[20]

HE INVESTS IN DEVELOPING LEADERS

To build a deep bench of these phenomenal team players, McNerney invests heavily in leadership development. He does this by spending a large amount of his own time developing leaders. He considers leadership development so important that he is willing to put relatively untested potential leaders in charge of major projects that could affect Boeing's future. The chance that those projects might fail can be thought of as a tuition payment by Boeing shareholders for developing Boeing's future leaders on the job. McNerney invests his time in training others, not only teaching in the corporate training center and exchanging ideas with employees through informal meetings, but also mentoring and empowering leaders.

At 3M, McNerney invested time in leadership development because he believed that it would help the company grow. His theory was that if he could help 3M's people grow, then the company would follow suit. "Leadership development is about helping people grow,"[21] McNerney has said, "and if I can get people as individuals growing, then I've got a company that grows." To do this, according to *Industry Week*, McNerney turned an R&D training center "at 3M Center in St. Paul into the Leadership Development Institute, a place where forty high-potential people at a time participated in the seventeen-day Accelerated Leadership Development Program. They would spend all seventeen days working on 3M problems selected by McNerney, and, as their training ended, share the solutions with him in a two-hour session. One team created a market-focused tool that was used in 3M's strategic planning process."[22]

McNerney also engages people outside the classroom in debates about the future. For example, at 3M he did "30 major events a year with 100 people or more." In those meetings he debated with people, pushed his ideas, told people what he was thinking about what the company was doing and why, and asked for feedback. McNerney created an environment that rewarded honest feedback instead of simply praising the boss's ideas.[23] By valuing 3Mers' ideas, McNerney sought to revitalize 3M after a decade of dormancy.

McNerney also personally spends time teaching at Boeing's Leadership Center in St. Louis. He does this in part so people will realize how important he thinks it is for them to follow the leadership attributes in pursuit of ever better results. McNerney also invests time in leadership development to let people know how he expects them to behave and to let them know that he will hold them accountable for meeting those expectations. In his words, "We're going to make sure people know we expect them to live by these attributes, both the performance and values nature of them. We are going to measure performance against them. We're going to tie career and job-readiness assessments to demonstrated progress in these areas. And we are going to insist that our leaders be models for the entire company of what the attributes are all about. As our people grow, so will Boeing."[24]

Outside the classroom, McNerney pushes his next generation of leaders to develop on the job. That's why he *empowers leaders*. He says that if he can get the "middle" of a company moving, growing, and aspiring to be leaders, then the company will grow and do well. To that end, McNerney shuns the hands-off approach of making the speech about leadership and then disappearing "into a backroom, grading everybody." Instead McNerney spends most of his time on people. As he says, that means thinking about "people issues broadly defined: Who's in what job? How do we accelerate this career? What programs do we have in place to train people? How do we make people fit better? How do we pay them? How do you differentiate pay?"[25]

To answer these questions, McNerney takes an active role in managing the careers of Boeing's future leaders. This means that he makes longer-term and higher-risk investments in people. He identifies the leaders who seem to have the most potential and gives them the authority and resources to make or break their piece of the company. According to Doug McVitie, a twenty-nine-year airline industry veteran, this willingness to invest in Boeing's future distinguishes McNerney from predecessors such as Phil Condit. As McVitie said, "Condit wanted to be the boss, at the top of the tree. So he made sure that the people below him were relative no-names. But McNerney is a pragmatic manager who is setting up the way forward for Boeing for the next thirty years. He knows that he's only one person and he needs to delegate. He can't do it all himself."[26]

McNerney creates the Boeing of the future by picking leaders for its 240 programs and other key jobs, and he "gives them room to breathe," says McVitie. This marks a change in attitude across Boeing and makes it a company that has, according to McVitie, "grown up and is a serious company in the new world. Rather than thinking it's the best and not trying very hard, as Boeing did under Condit and Stonecipher, McNerney is encouraging people to do as much as they can for themselves."[27]

In developing leaders, McNerney must balance delegation and control. If McNerney chooses a leader and leaves him or her to run a project without intervening at all, he could create a very entrepreneurial environment in which the leader could flourish. However, such a hands-off approach could lead to big problems if the project got into trouble. That trouble could be compounded if the leader did not exercise good judgment and withheld the bad news. So McNerney must choose carefully. He must pick a person he thinks can do the job, and then he must decide how much rope to give that person. If he provides too little rope, the person won't develop as a leader; too much rope increases the possibility of failure.

The delivery delays in the 787 program may be the result of too much rope. Specifically, McVitie concluded that McNerney may have trusted Bair too long in his role as head of the 787 program. As McVitie said, "Bair decided that it was more important to introduce the 787 on July 8, 2007, (7/8/07) than to get the plane built correctly. This led to the fiasco of forcing suppliers to provide a plane way before they were ready to do so. This 7/8/07 deadline was foisted on Bair by Marketing. Bair should have put his foot down. This decision forced Boeing to put a huge amount of pressure on its suppliers, for a nationalistic goal which was ironic for such an international aircraft. Under Condit, Bair would have been fired but McNerney moved him sideways."[28]

It is too soon to calculate the full cost to Boeing of McNerney's decision to trust Bair for too long. But his willingness to do so shows that McNerney views the idea of empowering leaders as a big investment in Boeing's future. While the Bair situation demonstrates that some of those investments can fail, McNerney believes that the benefits of investing in leadership development will ultimately prevail over its costs.

McNerney's investment in leadership development suggests four lessons:

- Spending time on leadership development gives the CEO the attention of key leaders and helps the CEO shape the way key leaders think about their jobs.
- Leadership development enables the CEO to create a shared sense of ownership about which behaviors result in rewards and which lead to being sidelined.
- Picking and empowering leaders prepares the company to prosper far into the future.
- The CEO must balance the desire to give leaders the freedom to succeed or fail against the need to protect shareholders from the cost of a failed project.

CONCLUSION

McNerney makes Boeing better by engaging its people in a purpose that captures their passion. He systematically dismantles the barriers that block people from achieving their goals. Specifically, he takes away the rewards for competing across functions and divisions; he unfreezes the flow of communication up and down the line; he wipes out systems that promote tenure over performance and political gamesmanship over delivering for customers and shareholders. He spends time working with people at the top and the middle of the organization to identify what needs to be changed and getting people to buy in to a set of shared leadership attributes. He then uses those attributes as a context in which to set goals and promote or sideline people based on their performance. By managing Boeing's talent pool, McNerney gives Wall Street the evidence it needs to have confidence in Boeing's future.

CHAPTER 2.

LEAD GROUPS
TO HIGHER GROUND

J ust as Jim McNerney motivates individual workers, he also
skillfully manages the various interest groups in the organizations he leads. In large organizations, there are many groups that
share common bonds but also compete for resources and rewards.
At Boeing, for example, McNerney has two large business units,
Boeing Integrated Defense Systems (IDS), which sells to the government, and Boeing Commercial Airplanes (BCA), which sells to
airlines. While they both have incentives to contribute the most
to Boeing's corporate profits, they serve different customers and
have their own engineering, manufacturing, and sales departments. Each of these departments has an identity as part of the
IDS or BCA team. Further, each also strongly identifies with its
own function within those larger teams. One of McNerney's big
jobs is to manage the relationships among these various units and
also between the company and the unions of its engineering and
manufacturing employees.

In order to boost Boeing's performance, McNerney needs to
do more than simply motivate the individuals in these groups. He
must also motivate these groups to cooperate with each other in
pursuit of Boeing's corporate aims. In doing this, McNerney faces

an important challenge, because the interests of these individual groups may sometimes be at odds with some of Boeing's overall corporate goals. Strategies, behaviors, or resource allocations that maximize the results of one unit might compete or interfere with the performance of another Boeing group. So when McNerney sets goals and pushes Boeing to devise and implement strategies, he must overcome the groups' natural desire to put their own interests above Boeing's.

McNerney does this, first of all, by pursuing corporate goals that make most groups better off. How does he accomplish this?

- He identifies the key players and understands their different needs.
- He focuses on getting agreement on critical issues and doesn't waste time on the trivial.
- He generates solutions that make key players better off.
- He overcomes obstacles to realize solutions.

HE IDENTIFIES THE KEY PLAYERS AND UNDERSTANDS THEIR DIFFERENT NEEDS

McNerney has a politician's ability to identify which constituents he needs to satisfy in order to help an organization move forward. In each situation, these constituents might be different, so it is important to figure out quickly who the important players are and how to relate to them in order to gain their support.

By maintaining a modest demeanor and not harshly condemning the status quo, McNerney puts himself in a good position to establish an initial rapport with these constituents. McNerney also listens carefully to their views, understands their goals, and appreciates the challenges they face in achieving those goals. With the input of these key groups, he forms a vision for action that enables him to pick goals that, if achieved, leave them all better off.

McNerney's shrewdness about leading people was evident as he stepped into Boeing as its CEO. McNerney had the experience from GE and 3M to realize that when a CEO joins an organization, he needs to gain the trust of the people in the organization. He inherits the history of conflicts among different groups and the frustration of those who thought they deserved his job. To keep these emotions from overwhelming his effectiveness, McNerney avoided charging into Boeing with lots of new ideas about how to fix everything that was wrong. Instead, he stepped into the new job quietly, praising Boeing's strengths and trying to get off on the right foot with its key constituents.

At Boeing, one of the key constituents was Boeing's machinists' union. When he became CEO, McNerney recognized that the union would test him to assess whether he was a confrontational negotiator like his immediate predecessor, Harry Stonecipher. The challenge for McNerney was to establish a different relationship with the machinists' union, shifting from a zero-sum to a plus-sum relationship between Boeing and the union. While Stonecipher had believed that in order for Boeing to win, the union had to lose (a zero-sum relationship), McNerney wanted to find a way for both Boeing and the union to end up better off (a plus-sum relationship).

In order to understand the needs of the machinists' union, as soon as he arrived McNerney quickly surveyed the political landscape. He used his skill to establish a good rapport with one of Boeing's key unions just two months after he became CEO. In August 2005 McNerney did something unexpected. He called Tom Buffenbarger, head of Boeing's International Association of Machinists and Aerospace Workers (IAM), after IAM's nineteen thousand members struck Boeing for a month. The strike had strained the relationship between McNerney and the union. Buffenbarger described the CEO as "an aloof kind of guy." But according to Buffenbarger, when McNerney called him, he suggested Boeing and the union should mend their relationship and work together on matters of mutual interest. This call led Buffenbarger to change his appraisal of McNerney, saying, "I think he's a realist and a pragmatist."[1]

Another key constituency for any incoming CEO is the incumbent executives who thought they should have gotten the CEO job. It is not difficult to imagine the smoldering resentment among these highly competitive and ambitious people who believed that they were far better qualified than the outsider to win the position. But incumbent executives are not simply resentful. They also fear that the new CEO will replace them with the CEO's own people. The incoming CEO must recognize that these experienced executives know far more about the company and, depending on their abilities and their willingness to work with the new CEO, could help the company succeed in the future.

McNerney demonstrated his ability to get off on the right foot with this constituency in his remarks to analysts and the media soon after he became Boeing's CEO. At a morning teleconference with analysts and media from corporate headquarters in Chicago, and in a phone interview later, McNerney acknowledged Boeing's struggles but spoke of a "bright future" and a company now poised to take off. He also bragged about Boeing's technical strength, saying, "The technology we have is awesome." Alan Mulally, who then headed BCA and was a contender for the CEO job and has been Ford's CEO since September 2006, liked what he heard. Mulally said, "I find it very interesting that he's talking about technical excellence . . . and using the technology to deliver value based on dynamite engineering and manufacturing. That tells everyone a lot about what drives" McNerney.[2]

When Welch decided that Jeff Immelt would succeed him as GE's CEO, he cleaned house by telling the losing candidates—McNerney and Robert Nardelli—that they had to leave GE. So by the time Immelt took office, McNerney and Nardelli were gone. By contrast, when McNerney became Boeing's CEO, the executives who had thought that they were candidates for that job were still there, and McNerney tried to keep them on board. For example, it was more than a year after McNerney became Boeing's CEO that Mulally left to become Ford's CEO.[3]

McNerney's actions reveal important lessons about how a leader should identify the key players in an organization and build relationships with them. Helpful tactics in this endeavor include:

- Start off by praising the company, its people, and its accomplishments;
- Avoid making major proclamations about how everything needs to change;
- Don't immediately replace the people who report to you; and
- Listen to key players before drawing conclusions about what needs to change.

HE FOCUSES ON GETTING AGREEMENT ON CRITICAL ISSUES AND DOESN'T WASTE TIME ON THE TRIVIAL

While it is important for a new leader to get off on the right foot with different constituents and to understand their needs, that alone is not sufficient to move an organization forward. One of the most challenging parts of a new leader's job is to figure out what tasks need to be accomplished first and how to convey the importance of those tasks to the various groups within the company. The leader must simultaneously decline to spend time on the many less important issues on which the different groups disagree.

Boeing's board hired McNerney precisely because it believed that his ability to identify those critical few goals efficiently was just what the company needed to clean up the mess his predecessors had left behind. Specifically, Boeing's board recognized that McNerney had the critical ability to navigate safely around corporate and political land mines.

McNerney used his navigational skill to tackle his first critical task: getting the right leaders into key jobs. McNerney reshuffled the organizational chart in a way that has added to Wall Street's confidence that Boeing will achieve more rapid earnings growth. According to Morgan Stanley's Heidi Wood, McNerney's ability to manage Boeing's talent translates directly into her confidence in forecasting its earnings results. As discussed in chapter 1, she notes that McNerney gets "phenomenally talented assholes" out of line management positions and puts phenomenally talented team players into the positions of leadership, sending the signal that the latter are more valuable to Boeing.[4]

Once McNerney achieved his goal of getting the right people into key jobs, he pulled them together as a team to choose Boeing's future direction from a range of possibilities that he outlined. The way he accomplished this was to engage people in the process of separating the critical few goals from the trivial many. When McNerney wants to develop a new strategy, for example, he gets people in a room and says, "Here are ten possible strategies. We're not leaving this room until we all agree on which one we're going to follow." Then McNerney gives people the authority to exercise their intellectual freedom. He encourages them to speak their minds. He demands debate. He lets them express their opinions without fear of retaliation.[5]

While they're speaking, McNerney listens intently and thoughtfully. The aircraft industry is very technologically sophisticated, and he recognizes that there are many people in the company who know the technology better than he does. So as he listens, he adjusts his proposals based on what he learns. This is one of the reasons that, unlike many CEOs, McNerney can operate without being perceived as the one issuing all the orders. When the meeting is over, McNerney says, "We all agreed that this is the right strategy. Okay, let's go do this together."

As a result, when people emerge from these strategy sessions, they believe that they, rather than McNerney, are the authors of Boeing's strategy. The result is a much greater sense of ownership, which pays off for Boeing when those people encounter seemingly insurmountable challenges to the strategy. Since they feel that the strategy is theirs—rather than one imposed on them by an imperious CEO—they are more likely to persevere until the strategy produces results. As Wood notes, "Ownership is inextricably linked to leadership."[6]

McNerney's ability to get key players to agree on a short list of goals is a valuable leadership skill. The skill benefits Boeing because McNerney and his team usually can identify the critical few goals the achievement of which will boost corporate performance. And since these high-impact goals are developed with input from the key players, McNerney does not have to force the goals on them.

HE GENERATES SOLUTIONS THAT MAKE KEY PLAYERS BETTER OFF

But exactly how does McNerney turn these goals into reality? He listens to what the constituents need and implements solutions that make the constituents better off while simultaneously accomplishing Boeing's aims. For Boeing's engineering union, McNerney did this by giving the unions a raise at a key plant, thereby averting a costly strike. This made the union happy that it could deliver higher pay to its members and benefited Boeing shareholders, who were spared the costs of a work stoppage. It also helped McNerney fulfill the predictions of a Wall Street analyst who put his reputation on the line by making an early positive call on Boeing stock. McNerney's quick settlement with the engineers rewarded the analyst by making him look prescient.

With the unions, McNerney found a solution that put him at odds—in a good way—with the union negotiating style of his predecessor, Harry Stonecipher. Stonecipher's dictatorial management style made many workers bristle. During a forty-day engineers' strike in 2000, union members stood on picket lines near a portable toilet labeled "Harry's Office." Workers felt that Stonecipher's leadership style was "all about power-based interactions and intimidation," according to Charles Bofferding, the former director of the Society of Professional Engineering Employees in Aerospace (SPEEA), a union that represents twenty-two thousand workers at Boeing and other companies.[7]

Months into McNerney's tenure as CEO, Bofferding had an opportunity to find out whether he would follow the same path as his predecessor or whether he'd take a different approach. McNerney and Bofferding were negotiating in November 2005 with 802 Boeing engineers. During those negotiations Bofferding e-mailed McNerney, who had then been Boeing's CEO for five months. Bofferding's e-mail asked whether Boeing's "negotiators' take-it-or-leave-it approach fit McNerney's vision for a new Boeing."[8]

Bofferding soon found out that the answer was no. When discussions resumed, Bofferding was startled by the change in tone. He recalls one negotiator saying, "I really want to hear what you have to say." And with the settlement, McNerney showed that he wanted to find a solution that would benefit Boeing and the union.[9]

In Bofferding's view, "McNerney is not a flamboyant, force-it-to-happen kind of guy. He's the efficient, help-it-to-happen -in-the-right-way sort." In the case of the SPEEA, what he helped happen was Boeing's December 2005 agreement to a 4 percent a year pay increase for its Wichita, Kansas–based engineers. The accord averted a walkout that would have come just after a month-long machinists' strike that had delayed $2 billion in orders. Mc-Nerney's use of power to get mutually beneficial results for workers and Boeing exemplifies his leadership style.[10] This ability to work with SPEEA may have contributed to a 9 percent rise in Boeing stock during McNerney's first six months as Boeing's CEO. That's because offering a raise without protracted negotiations removed a big uncertainty from Boeing's future earnings and established a basis for an effective working relationship between McNerney and its unions, which might avert future work stoppages.

Since the aircraft industry is so capital-intensive, McNerney realized that he needed to take particular care to meet the needs of another group, the Wall Street analysts who make recommendations about whether to buy or sell Boeing shares and who convey Boeing's story to investors. McNerney wanted to accelerate Boeing's earnings growth to reward the analysts who had confidence in him and to encourage others. The settlement with SPEEA contributed to that. For example, Byron Callan of Merrill Lynch had rated Boeing stock as "neutral" in the year preceding McNerney's takeover of the CEO position. However, the day McNerney was appointed, Callan upgraded Boeing to "buy" and said McNerney's appointment could lead to higher earnings. Such advice contributed to a quick 7 percent rise in Boeing stock.

But Callan recognized that intellectual capital and skills were the key to Boeing's longer-term success and that McNerney's talks with its unions would determine how well he could manage that capital.[11]

Callan's buy rating aligned his reputation as an early identifier of investment value with McNerney's ability to find a way to preside over more rapid earnings growth at Boeing. While Callan expected McNerney to act in a manner consistent with "the general reputation of people who come out of GE . . . that they do tend to run businesses by the numbers,"[12] he saw big challenges ahead at Boeing.

The strategic challenges Callan saw for Boeing would test McNerney's ability to grapple with a variety of issues. As Callan said, "Let's see how well the 787 goes. What really is going to happen with civil airplane demand? How do they correct these [ethics] issues that have bedeviled them on their large defense programs? It's not a cakewalk, but I feel pretty good about the person brought into this. In Boeing's context he's still a relatively young guy. He will leave his mark. Assuming he's there through his mid-60s, he should have a major role in shaping or reshaping Boeing." The settlement with SPEEA was an early signal that Callan's confidence in McNerney was well placed.[13]

As was consistent with one of the leadership attributes on Boeing's list—Find a Way—McNerney found a way. He found a way to give SPEEA the higher wages it wanted without increasing Boeing's labor costs so much that the company couldn't achieve the growth that Wall Street hoped to see. Indeed, this example illustrates how McNerney was able to find and implement a solution that made Boeing shareholders, its engineering employees, and Wall Street better off. If he had not settled with SPEEA, there might have been a long and widespread work stoppage. The residual distrust from such a strike, in turn, might have made future negotiations more difficult, to the detriment of both Boeing shareholders and the engineers.

HE OVERCOMES OBSTACLES
TO REALIZING SOLUTIONS

New strategies often undermine existing cultures and ways of doing business. This applies both within a company and in relations with customers and suppliers. So to put new strategies into practice, leaders must overcome resistance and inertia both within and outside the company. In 1997, when McNerney took over GE's Aircraft Engine Unit, he wanted GE to become the sole supplier of the engine for Boeing's 777. But he faced numerous obstacles to achieving that goal. Boeing was worried about the risks of depending on a single supplier, while the GE hierarchy was reluctant to make the investment in R&D needed to develop the engine that would meet Boeing's needs. And GE competitors Pratt & Whitney and Rolls-Royce had no interest in rolling over and letting McNerney eat their lunch. But McNerney overcame the obstacles and won the sole-source supply contract.

McNerney came up with the idea for the sole-source engine contract when GE's Aircraft Engine Unit was at a competitive disadvantage in the jet engine market—it was ranked third in the market for engines used in big twin-engine planes such as the Boeing 777. McNerney recognized an opportunity to overcome that competitive disadvantage by setting an ambitious goal of forging a sole-source supply agreement with Boeing that could catapult GE Aircraft Engines to the top of the market. McNerney had heard that Boeing, then a big GE customer, was planning longer-range models of the 777 that would require even more powerful engines. But thanks to its weak third-place position, GE was not eager to spend the $500 million it would take to develop the GE90—its engine for the longer-range model of the 777.[14] GE was reluctant to spend the money because it feared it would not sell enough engines to earn back its investment.

But McNerney was convinced that he could overcome the obstacles. That's because McNerney sensed that the long-range 777 would gain a sales advantage over the rival Airbus A340, a less fuel-efficient four-engine plane, according to Chuck Chadwell, a retired GE executive who worked in the unit. During dinner at Seattle's Four Seasons Hotel in early 1999, McNerney persuaded Mulally to pick a sole supplier for the new planes, Chadwell recalled. McNerney told Mulally that GE would invest in development costs and Boeing would save even more money because it would not need to certify the new model of the 777 for three different engines.

McNerney prevailed when Boeing chose GE later that year, shutting out Rolls-Royce and United Technologies' Pratt & Whitney division. The long-range 777s contributed significantly to Boeing's current sales success: In 1999 Boeing won 155 orders. The twenty-year exclusive contract with Boeing was valued at $25 billion for GE.[15] In Chadwell's view, without McNerney it would have been "four times harder to get the program off the ground."[16]

One of Boeing's objections to making GE a sole-source supplier, McNerney knew, was that Boeing executives were concerned that airlines that had never serviced GE engines before wouldn't want to take on such a risk. So McNerney called the heads of Singapore Airlines, Cathay Pacific Airways, and others and signed them up for his sole-sourcing idea by promising that GE would do everything it could to help maintain the engines. He also used GE's capital, promising to use its aircraft-leasing unit to buy the planes from Boeing and then lease them to airlines—if GE got an exclusive deal. And he enlisted Welch to personally lobby Boeing's then-CEO Phil Condit.

To appreciate the magnitude of McNerney's accomplishment, it's important to recognize what was at stake in this deal with Boeing. All the competitors in the engine market—GE, Pratt & Whitney, and Rolls-Royce—had concluded that the market for the new engine was not big enough to support three competitors with each investing the estimated $500 million needed to develop it. While GE and Pratt & Whitney went to Boeing and asked to be given the sole-source contract, Rolls-Royce agreed to build the engine with other suppliers. However, what would benefit the engine suppliers—the sole-source contract—would be to the disadvantage of the airlines because it would eliminate their ability to get a better value by playing the engine suppliers against each other.[17]

Through a combination of his personality and his understanding of what Boeing and its customers wanted, McNerney was able to offer a deal that persuaded Boeing to give the business to GE. According to one retired GE executive, McNerney is "one of the best, most well-rounded business managers there are. If there's a room full of people and Jim walks in there, you know he's somebody—he's confident. If he sits and talks with you, you will be as much at ease and taken by him."[18]

Ultimately, McNerney won by creating a vision that would simultaneously make Boeing better off, hurt GE's competition, and give GE's GE90 researchers the economic justification they needed to invest the $500 million required to build the engine. And just as important, McNerney was able to convince Boeing and GE's researchers, finance staff, and top executives that implementing his vision would make all of them better off. Thus, despite his lack of formal organizational power over any of them, McNerney was able to use his insights into their motivations to craft a strategy that was in their shared interest to implement.

Now that McNerney is Boeing's CEO, he encourages his

executives to overcome obstacles the way he did at GE Aircraft. He offers useful lessons:

- Give leaders the power to come up with ambitious goals, and knock away obstacles to realizing the goals.
- Teach leaders to recognize why key players might resist some goals.
- Help leaders devise creative ways to overcome that resistance.
- Encourage leaders to use the CEO to help close deals and get access to resources needed to achieve the goals.

CONCLUSION

McNerney's ability to lead groups to higher ground marks him as an exceptional leader. He demonstrates organizational savvy in his ability to take over a new organization without fanning the flames of envy or incurring the wrath of rival internal tribes. Instead, he praises the company and helps people see that their future may be brighter thanks to his leadership. By creating this openness, McNerney learns what most urgently needs to be done and unites different groups around those critical goals. From this unity, he crafts workable strategies to achieve the goals, and he has demonstrated the persistence and resourcefulness to overcome obstacles that might block the implementation of these strategies. Thanks to his ability to satisfy the interests of various constituencies, McNerney excels at boosting the performance of complex organizations.

CHAPTER 3.

LINK PAY TO PROFIT AND PROCESS, NOT STOCK PRICE

During the 1980s, when a wave of junk bond–fueled acquisitions highlighted the gap between companies' low stock prices and their higher asset values, the phrase "shareholder value" became a Wall Street buzzword. Many investors felt that executives were not sufficiently concerned about investor returns, and began clamoring for changes in how executives were compensated. So, by the end of the 1990s, the compensation of most executives was tied directly to the value of their company's stock.

The theory was that basing executives' pay on the stock price would focus the attention of the people running the company on better performance. But, while there is a connection between a company's financial performance and its stock price, the connection isn't always that firm and clear. As a result, it turned out that executives were being compensated, or not compensated, for something that was essentially out of their control.

There are certainly theories that connect a firm's financial performance to the way investors should value a company. But those theories relate the present value of future cash flows to the price investors should be willing to pay. And despite their best efforts, no executive can forecast accurately how much money any company is going to make in the future.

Nor, for that matter, can executives control another factor critically important to the value of a firm's stock—the expectations of Wall Street analysts. If a company can exceed their expectations and raise its guidance for future growth, then the odds are strong that the stock will rise. But the instant a company reports quarterly results that are weaker than analysts were expecting, or lowers its growth forecast, investors sell. If they ask questions, they ask them only later, after they have tanked the stock.

Because managers can't control their companies' stock price, Jim McNerney believes it is inappropriate to pay them based on stock price performance alone. Some executives may try to control stock prices. Executives at Enron and WorldCom were spurred to manipulate their companies' financial results in order to boost their own personal net worth. But in the end, they killed the companies.

So rather than compensate executives for things they can't control, McNerney ties compensation to what managers can control. He pays them to focus their efforts on the financial performance that's under their control and in the company's long-term interests. To accomplish this, McNerney does the following things:

- He bases pay on factors that leaders can control.
- He weighs both profit and process.
- He makes shareholder value a by-product.

HE BASES PAY ON FACTORS THAT LEADERS CAN CONTROL

McNerney uses a measure called **economic profit** as the gauge of executive performance. This concept of economic profit distills finance theory into a relatively simple formula that he uses to determine how much bonus to pay business unit leaders. Specifically,

McNerney believes that leaders should be able to control two variables in their businesses: how much *profit* they earn and how much *capital* they use to achieve those profits. His notion is that the best business leaders make efficient use of the company's capital. For example, it's better for a business unit to earn $100 million of profit using $10 million of capital than to generate that same $100 million in profit but require $50 million of capital to get it.

In McNerney's view, profit and capital are completely under the control of business unit leaders, and he expects them to take full responsibility for how well they manage these factors. A corollary of this responsibility is that leaders will not try to make excuses if they do not meet their performance targets. After all, if McNerney expects them to be able to control profits and capital, such hand waving would make them appear less competent.

McNerney also concentrates on these two factors because he believes that *over the long run*, investors will pay a premium for a company's shares if its business units consistently achieve high return on capital. In focusing leaders on return on capital rather than short-term profits, McNerney wants to eliminate any incentives for business unit leaders to make decisions that might just boost short-term earnings to please Wall Street. McNerney's focus on paying bonuses to business unit leaders who maximize return on capital over the long run is intended to focus them on the long-term health of the company.

At Boeing, McNerney uses the new Annual Incentive Plan bonuses based on a formula that takes into account the overall company performance—a **company** score—and each executive's score against preset performance targets—the **individual** score. Boeing's **company score** ranges between 0.0 (unacceptable) and 2.0 (outstanding). For 2006, the company score was 1.2 because it was above the target of 1.0 and made more economic profit after adjustments than expected. Boeing's 1.2 company score reflected its "double-digit revenue growth, continued productivity improvements and record commercial airplane orders and total backlog which impacted cash flow and net assets."[1]

There was, however, one executive who took a big compensation hit in 2006. As head of the Integrated Defense Systems unit, James Albaugh saw his bonus fall 54 percent from $1.6 million in 2005 to $730,000 in 2006. Albaugh got the same score as all of Boeing's top executives on the company's overall performance, but he took the hit because he received a weak individual score.[2]

In 2006, IDS's poor performance on a military project—the 737 Airborne Warning and Control System (AWACS) program—resulted in a $274 million charge and sliced IDS profits by 2.4 percent. In reducing Albaugh's 2006 bonus, McNerney was making it clear that he held him accountable for the AWACS program's problems and their negative impact on Boeing's earnings.[3]

Conversely, McNerney cuts executives slack when it comes to costs outside their control. That leniency was reflected in the decision to exclude from the 2006 performance calculation two big charges for the year: $571 million paid to the federal government to settle all legal cases related to two defense-procurement scandals; and $320 million to terminate Boeing's failed Connexion in-flight Internet venture. Since the committee believed that current Boeing executives were not responsible for these charges, it excluded them from consideration in setting those executives' bonuses.[4]

McNerney pays people based on factors that they can control because it leads to better corporate performance. Specifically, his approach to pay provides the following benefits:

- **Creates accountability.** It makes managers accountable for factors they should be able to control—the operating profit each quarter and the cost of the capital they use to generate that profit.

- **Minimizes room for excuses.** By defining profit as net operating income, it excludes corporate charges that the managers don't control. This lowers the opportunity for managers to make excuses if they don't meet performance standards.
- **Draws on finance theory.** McNerney applies the basic finance concept that businesses in a portfolio need to earn more than the corporate cost of capital.
- **Rewards managers who hit the target.** It offers substantial profit sharing to managers who meet their targets—a by-product of which, McNerney believes, is greater shareholder value.

HE WEIGHS BOTH PROFIT AND PROCESS

While achieving economic profit and other business unit goals is clearly important to McNerney, he believes that it is equally important **how** people achieve those goals. Process matters to McNerney. He does not want people who meet all the sales goals but do so in a way that violates Boeing's values. We saw in chapter 1 how McNerney works with people to define leadership attributes. And these attributes provide people with clear signals about what kind of behavior McNerney wants to see from his people as they strive to achieve business goals. The compensation systems he designs reinforce the leadership attributes.

He tailors his approach to each company according to the values that he feels he needs to reinforce. For example, when he arrived at 3M, he decided he needed to set far more ambitious financial targets than his predecessor had set. But as he was doing that, he had to tackle two problems with 3M's culture. First, people were very set in their ways, and second, those ways were sluggish and complacent. McNerney recognized that in order to get 3M to achieve the faster growth goals he set, he would need to change the way 3M people worked. To do that, he specified the kinds of profit and process he hoped they would produce.

However, just as process mattered to McNerney in evaluating leaders, McNerney's own process for managing the change mattered to 3M's people. Specifically, if McNerney had charged in and started issuing orders to double earnings growth or to take more initiative, it is likely that it wouldn't have worked. At worst, the veteran 3Mers could have resisted and sabotaged his efforts. At best, they would have bristled at his efforts to boost performance, especially if he made big demands without offering any guidance about how to achieve them.

To motivate employees in pursuit of these performance goals, McNerney tried to create a bright vision of the future. Bob Burgstahler, 3M senior vice president of business development and corporate services, said about McNerney's numerous meetings with employees: "Jim doesn't say, 'You've got to do this.' Instead he says, '3M has this tremendous reputation and global presence and great technology, and I see all these opportunities we can leverage if we get on the same page and help each other.' "[5]

When McNerney joined 3M, he found that people made decisions slowly and projects moved slowly. 3M also lacked disciplined performance reviews and accountability. Its pay-for-performance incentive system had deteriorated into a form of entitlement.

McNerney toughened up the incentive system by tying a large percentage of pay to economic profit and achievement of operating targets. Besides improving accountability, it helped McNerney identify people who had high potential. He channeled these people into leadership development programs where they began to set a faster pace for others.[6]

But to discover these people and provide them with compelling opportunities, McNerney needed to resolve a powerful tension at 3M between its younger workers and its old-timers. These

3M veterans had never worked anywhere but 3M, and they were quite comfortable with a system that rewarded them for tenure. But its anemic performance frustrated 3M's younger generation of workers. They had a strong desire to innovate and contribute to more rapid growth, but 3M's bureaucratic environment stifled them.

McNerney tilted the playing field in favor of those workers who wanted to accelerate 3M's growth. To do that, he required 3M's managers to rank every employee reporting to them, a 3M version of GE's "rank and yank." McNerney and his top lieutenants tried to gain acceptance for the new grading system by reminding employees that in past surveys they had complained that underperformers were too protected at 3M. Under McNerney's predecessor, for example, all managers above a certain level at 3M received stock options each year.[7]

McNerney used the rankings to allocate 3M stock options. Under McNerney's new plan, options were granted only to those with better-than-average performance grades. As McNerney put it, "3M had a tendency to overvalue experience and undervalue leadership." Aggressive young employees liked the new system. In the past, they had had to climb a ladder of narrowly defined jobs. McNerney's new system encouraged them to step out of these career nooks and even jump over weakly performing veteran employees.[8]

By awarding more stock options to those who took initiative, McNerney signaled the kind of behavior he would reward at 3M and what behavior he would punish. McNerney's new ranking and pay approach excited people with leadership ambitions and potential. Conversely, it made the weaker veteran employees feel left out and it encouraged them to depart.

When McNerney arrived at Boeing, he used a similar process to rank managers. However, McNerney believed that Boeing had a different set of cultural problems. Whereas 3M suffered from lethargy because of a system that rewarded tenure over performance, Boeing's big problem was a culture that cast a blind eye on ethics and let managers treat subordinates roughly to achieve financial goals.

McNerney took a different approach to ranking people at Boeing. He wanted to change the behavior of Boeing's managers. He believed that they, rather than the workers, were the source of many of the problems, so he asked employees to assess their managers. By doing this, he let managers know that if they treated employees roughly, he would limit their opportunities within Boeing. Specifically, McNerney required subordinates to rank Boeing managers on how well they "inspire others" and "reflect Boeing values." McNerney ended the careers of those who only measured up well on "delivers results," without living Boeing's values.[9]

McNerney weighs profit and process in deciding how much to pay people because he takes the longer-term view that it's more important to get results in a way that will enable Boeing to prosper far into the future. The way he does this suggests several lessons for leaders:

- It is dangerous to measure leaders simply on financial outcomes because it risks encouraging behavior that trades away long-term value creation to achieve short-term results.
- Process matters when trying to change how performance is measured—it's important not to alienate people by pushing too hard or too fast for radical change.
- Leaders should tailor how they change profit and process measures to each company.
- Process and profit are not mutually exclusive; rather, process is a *leading indicator* of profit—that is, if leaders stress the

right values, people will behave in a way that generates superior profitability.

HE MAKES SHAREHOLDER VALUE A BY-PRODUCT

McNerney encourages people not to focus too much attention on a company's stock price. Whereas his predecessors at Boeing linked bonuses to stock price increases, McNerney decided it was better to focus executives' attention on the variables within a manager's control. If executives meet their economic profit targets while adhering to corporate values, they receive bonuses regardless of stock price performance.

While McNerney fully understands his responsibility to increase shareholder value, he also realizes that in the aircraft industry, which has long product development cycles, it would be a mistake to focus too much on quarterly results. McNerney's theory is that if Boeing makes the right long-term investments in new projects and meets its milestones, shareholder value will take care of itself. That is the reason McNerney changed Boeing's financial incentives. Boeing's pre-McNerney long-term incentive system, called Performance Shares, paid out based on a higher stock price. But that system failed to consider management's performance during the down cycles inherent in the industry, thus offering managers few incentives to find a way to improve performance during a downturn over which they had no control.[10] Nevertheless, McNerney saw many motivational benefits to making Boeing stock an important part of the executive compensation program. Moreover, McNerney did not reject all aspects of Boeing's compensation program. In fact, he found at least one aspect of Boeing's program, the one that required Boeing executives to buy more stock as they rose through the ranks, quite useful. So he continued it after he became CEO.

McNerney thought it was important for Boeing executives to buy shares because it:

- **Encourages higher-ranking people to own more stock.** As an employee rises up into Boeing's executive ranks, McNerney expects that person to align his or her career and personal financial interests with those of Boeing shareholders.
- **Drives corporate, not parochial, actions.** It motivates executives to do what is in Boeing's corporate interest rather than what benefits solely their specific department.
- **Aligns management and shareholder interests.** It tells Boeing's shareholders that its top executives have skin in the same game they do. They will benefit if the stock rises and will suffer if it falls.
- **Motivates long-term focus.** It reinforces McNerney's philosophy that if leaders achieve the company and individual goals he sets for them, they will benefit over the long run through the greater value of their Boeing shares.

So what is this program? Started in 1998—well before McNerney became CEO—the stock purchase program is based on a multiple of base salary tied to executive grade. The stock ownership guidelines require that, within a three-year period, Boeing executives reach and maintain an investment position in Boeing stock at levels that rise with their rank, as follows:

- **CEO:** six times base salary
- **Executive vice presidents and senior vice presidents:** four times base salary
- **Vice presidents:** between one and two times base salary[11]

The key element here is that the executives must hold on to the shares. McNerney wants his executives to share the motivations of long-term Boeing shareholders. The higher they rise within the company, the more of their own money he requires them to invest. In imposing this requirement, McNerney aims to discourage executive decisions that might boost earnings in the short term while sacrificing Boeing's longer-term value or reputation. More important, McNerney wants to encourage these executives to boost Boeing's long-term value by behaving in the interests of the whole corporation, and not just of their own operating units.

CONCLUSION

McNerney's approach to paying leaders seeks to get them to do the right things in the right way. Focusing managers on what they can control means that they spend less time squabbling about matters that do not benefit shareholders and customers. This, in and of itself, can enhance corporate productivity. The focus on process, not results alone, means that it's easier to attract and motivate top people. As an added benefit, legal and regulatory problems are likely to fall as well. Moreover, if McNerney is correct that Wall Street will reward companies that earn profits in excess of their cost of capital, then compensating leaders for achieving corporate and individual goals will pay off for shareholders.

CHAPTER 4.

BUILD STRATEGY
ON CUSTOMER FOCUS

There was a time in the not-so-distant past when the key to market victory in a technology-intensive industry was to hire engineers, throw them in a room, and let them invent the future of your business. That approach has lost its currency over the last couple of decades. That may be because many formerly prominent technology companies have been wiped out by following it. Digital Equipment Corporation (DEC), for example, a $14 billion company employing over seventy-seven thousand people, took that approach, stumbled badly, and was ultimately acquired by Compaq, which in turn was bought by Hewlett Packard.

DEC's engineers created a company that dominated the market for minicomputers. These multiuser computers were smaller than big mainframes and were quite popular for a while. Then, in the early 1980s, the personal computer began to steal the market. But DEC's CEO, Ken Olsen, who had helped invent the minicomputer, did not really understand why anybody would want to use a PC, which someone else discovered. So DEC didn't respond, while its customers looked for ways to create systems of PCs networked together rather than buying more of DEC's minicomputers. Eventually, Olsen left the company, but his successor could not revive it, so its directors ultimately sold it to Compaq.

What does this story have to do with Boeing and Jim McNerney? During his career at GE, 3M, and Boeing, McNerney, who is not an engineer, has learned that technology is valuable but alone it is not enough to sustain the growth of a successful technology company. The company must use the technology to do things that the customers want. McNerney sustains companies' success by investing in technology that meets customer needs better than competitors and cutting off funds for technology that he sees as merely an engineer's hobby.

When it comes to managing technology, McNerney pleases the customers instead of pleasing the engineers. He doesn't let the engineers isolate themselves in their labs. He encourages them to work with their counterparts in other departments, such as purchasing, manufacturing, finance, and sales, to find the technologies and the uses for technology that are most beneficial to the company and to its customers. He also encourages these cross-functional teams to spend time with customers so they can understand what products they need to offer in order to close future sales.[1]

McNerney's winning approach is to build strategy on customer focus, which he does in the following ways:

- He forms teams from different functions and across corporate boundaries.
- He satisfies the needs of customers, not engineers.
- He harnesses technologies that will make customers better off.
- He shifts resources to projects with the highest profit potential.

HE FORMS TEAMS FROM DIFFERENT FUNCTIONS
AND ACROSS CORPORATE BOUNDARIES

McNerney's actions at GE, 3M, and Boeing show that he understands the business peril associated with engineers developing new products in isolation. He has teamed up engineers with people from other departments, such as sales, manufacturing, purchasing, and finance. Moreover, he has encouraged them to work with people outside the firm, including customers and suppliers, in order to speed up the delivery of products in a highly competitive marketplace.

McNerney says he has observed that when programs fail, teamwork is generally absent. He has found that failure in developing new products is often the result of leadership that encourages each business function to compete with the others. This competition often results in engineers designing products that are difficult to manufacture and sell. This leadership approach also often drives the company to satisfy internal goals rather than to help customers and reach for market share.

As McNerney sees it, internal competition creates the illusion of success when each function perceives that it did what was needed to make its leaders look good, even though the project failed. According to McNerney, "Too many programs flame out with two-thirds of the people feeling like, 'Well, I did my job.' When a program flames out, everybody in the program ought to feel that as a team they didn't succeed. That only comes from everybody helping each other, people unafraid to offer views to the person next to them and to someone above them. That climate has to be created at the top."[2]

In his efforts to create that kind of climate, McNerney engages people in a dialogue that pits what he calls *innovation myths*—which are the source of the problems mentioned above—against *innovation* **realities.** The myths that McNerney seeks to destroy are the ones that enshrine innovation as the province of the lone technologist developing a breakthrough idea. McNerney's innovation reality is that success springs from teams consisting of people from both inside and outside a company working together to improve products in a disciplined way to benefit customers.

McNerney cites five myths of innovation that need to be overcome by individuals "as they seek to contribute creatively in the modern corporate environment." These five harmful myths include:

- **Innovation is a crusade.** The iconic, classic crusading researcher is responsible for most innovation.
  - Companies that accept this myth become too dependent on idiosyncratic individuals who demand resources, often fail to communicate their progress, and work poorly with others.
- **Innovation is technology alone.** Innovation is all about technology, and technologists are the only innovators.
  - This myth undervalues the importance in a large company of the different functions that are needed to take an idea and turn it into a profit-making product line.
- **All innovation is radical.** Innovation has to change everything.
  - This myth is dangerous because it focuses people only on big breakthrough innovations, which occur rarely, and does not encourage the smaller technological improvements that are often most valuable to a company's current customers.
- **Innovation is lucky.** Innovation is a matter of serendipity or accidental luck.
  - While luck plays a role in innovation, the notion that it's all

about luck tends to undervalue the benefit of making many frugal choices, of doing experiments and quickly culling failures, and of working to improve the odds of success.

- **Innovation must be undisciplined.** Discipline and creativity are mortal enemies and cannot coexist.
  - The danger of this myth is that it puts too much control into the hands of a lone technologist who may be unwilling to give up on a failing project. This starves the company of resources for projects with greater profit potential.[3]

McNerney contrasts these five *myths* with five *innovation realities*:

- **Innovation requires teaming.** Innovation is a team, not a solo, sport.
  - Working alone might be okay for an individual trying to start a business, but in a corporate environment, different functions must work together and companies must team up with their suppliers and customers. The benefit of such teaming is that it leads to products that are easier to manufacture, sell, distribute, and service.
- **Innovation is shared.** Innovation depends on a culture of technical sharing and openness to others, not a reclusive environment.
  - If teams share information about new products, they can identify and fix problems early in the process, which saves money and time. Hoarding information leads to costly delays and rework because it uncovers problems after too much time and money have been spent.
- **Innovation is broad.** Innovation can and should occur in all areas of the business.
  - McNerney expects all functions of a business to look for

ways to improve. He believes that isolating innovation in one department limits opportunities for improvement.

- **Innovation can be incremental.** Incremental doesn't mean insignificant, and eureka moments are rare.
  - McNerney values innovation that results in incremental performance improvements because those improvements can help a company outperform competitors and boost market share. Moreover, McNerney believes that if a company measures innovation success solely on the basis of how many breakthroughs it creates, then the rarity of such breakthroughs will frustrate the company.
- **Innovation must combine creativity and discipline.** In a business environment, creativity cannot exist without discipline.
  - McNerney believes that creativity for which customers are willing to pay can only have the resources it needs if a company has the discipline to reallocate capital and people from failing or irrelevant programs to winning ones.

McNerney believes that replacing the myths with the realities can only happen with strong leadership. As he put it, "It takes people working together across different groups, disciplines, and organizational arms to make it happen. It also takes real leadership to chart the course and [inspire] people to reach for the highest level of performance supported by a never ending focus on integrity."[4]

To help companies make the transition from the five myths to the five realities, McNerney believes that leaders must acculturate engineers and manage them to behave differently. Specifically, he pushes engineers to work well with others. To that end, he encourages engineers to "build their communication and interpersonal skills, work collaboratively with other people, listen attentively, and convey information clearly, succinctly, and persuasively."[5]

McNerney sees the 787 as an example of a successful cross-functional innovation. Despite problems in meeting its production schedule due to a failure to manage effectively relationships with suppliers (a lapse we'll examine in chapter 9), the 787 has generated a record number of orders prior to delivery. And one of the reasons for the 787's popularity, in McNerney's view, was the way that Boeing teams worked together to create a product that customers wanted. Boeing's marketing department researched demand and communicated to Boeing's engineers and business leaders what customers wanted. Then Boeing used advances in technology to cater to the needs of its customers.

HE SATISFIES THE NEEDS OF CUSTOMERS, NOT ENGINEERS

Engineers are the magic ingredient of most technology companies. But the way they deliver their magic has changed in recent years. At Digital Equipment, the engineers ruled, and the company eventually failed because of that. Engineers often still rule in companies that create new markets and grab market share by introducing breakthrough technologies. However, the airline industry is no longer that kind of market. Unlike at the beginning of the twentieth century, when the airline industry was just getting started, it's not possible for an ambitious engineering graduate to start up an aircraft manufacturer. Since the capital requirements for commercializing it are so high, only a large company can afford to develop a technical breakthrough in the aircraft industry. And the successful commercialization of the breakthrough will only happen if engineers coordinate effectively with many different functions both within the aircraft manufacturer and outside with suppliers and customers. In short, aerospace engineers cannot succeed working alone.

At Boeing, engineers still play a critical role. However, that role has changed in a way that boosts the chances that Boeing aircraft will meet its customers' needs and generate orders. The fundamental shift in the role of engineers is from one that focuses inward to one that emphasizes how engineers, as members of the product development team, can design, build, deliver, and service an aircraft that helps Boeing customers compete more effectively.

Teaching engineers to accept this new role is essential in order to succeed in making the transition from the world of the five myths to that of the five realities. Instead of being the sole source of innovation, engineers must see themselves as part of a team whose mission is to create products that satisfy unmet customer needs. McNerney believes this transition is important because he has seen that engineers who work only on technologies that interest them and their peers often create products that do not meet the needs of customers. If engineers could invent entirely new markets—an increasingly rare event in a world with intense global competition—then such an approach might make sense. However, McNerney sees incremental innovation as the norm, and in his view, this requires engineers and others on the cross-functional team to listen to customers, which in Boeing's case includes **airlines** *and* airline **passengers**.

When McNerney arrived, Boeing already had one big project that used the customer-centric design process, the 787. While the design was a model of teamwork, the delivery was not. In particular, the 787 delivery problems were due in part to the insistence by Boeing's marketing department that a display version of the 787 be rushed in front of the public in the summer of 2007 (7/8/07) even though Boeing suppliers told the marketers that their target delivery date was unrealistic. This example suggests that it can be a mistake for a decision maker to ignore the protests of product development team members—in this case Boeing suppliers—because a single function is pushing so hard for its own interests. If Boeing had listened to these suppliers more closely, it would have realized that what its marketers wanted was not in its customers' best interests. In retrospect, it would have been better if Boeing had delayed the 787 rollout until all members of the product development team thought it was ready.

Nevertheless, when McNerney became CEO in 2005, the production problems were still ahead of Boeing. At that time, McNerney was quick to praise Mulally for putting the customer at the center of the 787 design process. In McNerney's view, Mulally saw that the airline industry had changed and pushed Boeing to develop the 787 to help the airlines compete in that new world. Specifically, Mulally saw that from the airlines' perspective, the world had become more security-conscious and passengers wanted to limit the number of times they got on and off airplanes. Further, oil prices were rising and not expected to decline. Controlling maintenance costs and passenger convenience were also important. Finally, in light of their cost pressures, Mulally understood that airlines were seeking ways to improve their productivity.[6]

In McNerney's view, the 787's design process was a model of how to build an aircraft that focused the technology skills of engineers on creating value for customers. Or as he put it, the 787 was a successful engineering feat that began with the marketplace. Specifically, the 787 would enable airlines to charge lower fares, offer more direct flights, deliver more space on long flights, provide the highest comfort level, and operate more nonstop flights at significantly reduced operating costs. Moreover, the 787 would use 20 percent less fuel and cost 30 percent less to maintain than the competitor's products.[7] These specific benefits resulted from what McNerney saw as the appropriate marriage between the role of engineers as the source of new technology and the needs of Boeing customers to compete in a changed world.

Much of the technology for the 787 was borrowed from a project that failed because it didn't take customer needs sufficiently into account. The earlier aircraft, known as the Sonic Cruiser, was designed to fly more quickly because that's what Boeing's engineers thought a plane should do, but it turned out that that wasn't what the customers wanted. According to a retired GE executive who was familiar with the project, the Sonic Cruiser, which used composite materials, "was an engineer's dream—it was like the DeLorean [a slick sports car developed during the 1980s that generated insufficient sales and ultimately failed]. When salespeople tried to sell the Sonic Cruiser, the airlines weren't interested, and Boeing scrapped the program."[8]

Having scrapped the Sonic Cruiser, Boeing wanted its replacement—the 787—to benefit from deep insights into its customers' customer—the airline passenger. Boeing sought to learn what passengers wanted by interviewing twenty thousand people. It decided that such interviews would help Boeing to rethink the experience of flying from the passenger's perspective. Among other things, in its interviews Boeing asked passengers to write essays about their first flight experience and their most recent one. Boeing found that people's memories of their first flight experience tended to be pleasant, while their most recent experience was awful. People complained that they felt like convicts going through the airport screening, there was no food on the plane, and they felt as though they were traveling on an inner city bus.[9]

Boeing's 787 design team also drew lessons from the world of animal behavior. According to Wood, animals feel fear when they can't see clearly around them. Boeing wanted to eliminate this problem through a seating plan that enabled people to see all around them. Further, Wood notes that the 787's air is filtered and far moister than the air in aluminum aircraft. (Aluminum aircraft need to fly at higher altitudes to avoid getting wet, which would cause them to rust and corrode. At higher altitudes, the aircraft cabin humidity drops.) The result is that people will not get as dehydrated, which is a major cause of jet lag. So passengers will feel better while they're on the flight and after they arrive at their destination.[10]

HE HARNESSES TECHNOLOGIES THAT WILL MAKE CUSTOMERS BETTER OFF

Technology alone does not make a company successful. For example, if Boeing had tried to sell, build, and deliver the Sonic Cruiser, there's a very good chance that it would not have recouped its development costs. Boeing would not have sold enough Sonic Cruisers because airlines did not want an aircraft that flew near the speed of sound. Cutting the time from takeoff to landing was not the issue that kept airline executives up at night, so an aircraft like the Sonic Cruiser was not going to help them compete.

Instead, the airline industry needed an aircraft that excelled in different areas. For example, the airline industry was finding that competitors such as Southwest Airlines, which flew direct flights between out-of-the-way airports, made more money than airlines like United that flew into hubs such as Chicago and required passengers to wait there until their connecting flight could depart. The price of jet fuel, airlines' second-largest cost, was rising rapidly, which slashed airlines' profitability. To help airlines save money, Boeing decided to funnel the composite technology used in the Sonic Cruiser into a different kind of aircraft that would meet the airlines' need for an aircraft that required less fuel and could fly those direct routes more efficiently.

This process of matching up new technologies to solve customers' problems is a leadership skill that McNerney applied at

GE and Boeing. As we saw in chapter 2, when McNerney sold jet engines at GE, he was able to get GE to invest $500 million in a new, more fuel-efficient jet engine that would create a compelling economic incentive for his then customer, Boeing, to buy all the engines for its new 777 jet from GE. The value of that victory for GE was enormous—in 1999 McNerney estimated it to "eventually be worth $15 billion or more to GE over the [next] two decades."[11] But as we saw in chapter 2, he underestimated the deal's value by $10 billion. Here are two major reasons that GE won this contract:

- McNerney understood the engine performance characteristics that Boeing wanted for its long-range 777 models.
- McNerney persuaded GE to invest in the technologies needed to deliver an engine, the GE90, that would satisfy those performance requirements.

McNerney spent a significant amount of time with Boeing to understand what it was looking for in an engine for the long-range 777. Boeing told him it was looking for a plane with a *higher take-off weight* and *longer range*. To satisfy these needs, Boeing wanted to build an aircraft that could carry three hundred passengers and have a maximum range of 10,100 statutory miles—1,200 more than Boeing's shorter-range model.[12]

Based on his understanding of these needs, McNerney pushed GE to invest $500 million to build an engine that would meet Boeing's needs for this long-range 777. That investment led GE to build and test prototypes that helped persuade Boeing that GE could design, manufacture, build, test, and certify the engine in twenty-four months. These tests demonstrated to Boeing that the GE90 would be able to meet its stringent performance criteria.

How did McNerney harness technology to make customers

better off? GE tested a new compressor and new engine blades that would be able to meet the demands of Boeing's long-range 777. GE ground tested an increased-operating-temperature, improved-efficiency, high-pressure compressor that would enable the long-range 777 to take off with more passengers and to fly farther. GE also developed and tested new fan blades for the GE90. These tests helped persuade Boeing that GE would be able to deliver an engine that satisfied the performance characteristics of its long-range 777.[13]

McNerney pushes his people at Boeing to use this same approach, to match new technologies to customer needs. McNerney encourages R&D to think about how Boeing's aircraft technology can help airlines compete. McNerney's role in this process is evident in the way he interacts with Boeing's chief technology officer, James M. Jamieson. Specifically, Jamieson observes, McNerney "looks down into the details and brings it (technology) up to a high level of strategy." Jamieson recalls how McNerney once asked him to explain the benefits of the composite technology being used on the 787. Jamieson started explaining about the longer fatigue life of composites and the lack of corrosion compared with aluminum, until McNerney stopped him. "I was giving him a pure technical answer, and he was asking what it means to business, the passenger, and the airlines," Jamieson says. "He's asking the broader questions. He has objectivity because he wasn't raised in one of our worlds."[14]

McNerney encouraged Boeing to make engineering breakthroughs in the 787 that would satisfy the performance improvement standards that airlines demanded. Specifically, McNerney noted that the 787's innovations include the use of a one-piece composite fuselage, composite wings, and a more advanced engine. These new technologies result in a lighter aircraft that should be less expensive to maintain. The composite materials provide greater strength per pound than other materials. Moreover, the one-piece composite fuselage eliminates the use of 1,500 aluminum sheets, their hanging elements, and fifty thousand fasteners.[15]

McNerney praises the way Boeing made the transition in its design process from the *engineering-driven* Sonic Cruiser to the *customer-need-driven* 787. McNerney holds up as a model the way that Boeing used much of that Sonic Cruiser technology to meet the newly recognized needs of its airline customers. Within sixty days of canceling the Sonic Cruiser, Boeing had learned from talking with airlines that they would be willing to buy an aircraft that flew directly to destinations rather than to hubs—a "point-to-point" aircraft—made from composite materials. The use of composite materials would create a virtuous cycle for an aircraft targeted at that market—composites were lighter, which would save aircraft weight and cost. This would mean that it required a lighter engine, which would produce less thrust at takeoff. And the lower takeoff thrust would mean the aircraft would use less fuel—thus making it lighter. This logic persuaded Boeing to transfer hundreds of people—with their composite technology expertise—from the Sonic Cruiser to the 787.[16]

McNerney's approach to harnessing technologies that make customers better off demonstrates three leadership lessons:

- **Listen to your customers and their customers.** Boeing sells to many different groups of customers. It sells aircraft directly to airlines, but it sells indirectly to the passengers that the airlines are battling to attract. In order to help the airlines win that competitive battle, Boeing recognized that it needed to listen to both sets of customers and understand their unmet needs in a deep way.
- **Leaders must match technology to these customer needs.**

Technology innovation for the sake of satisfying engineers is not sufficient. However, as the Sonic Cruiser example suggests, leaders can repurpose such technology to help create new products that better meet a customer's needs. And by doing that, the company can win more business.

- **Leaders must understand how these technologies can interact to benefit customers.** In applying new technologies, leaders need to recognize how various new technologies will interact with each other to create diverse benefits for customers and customers' customers. The 787's composite materials helped increase fuel efficiency by creating a lighter aircraft while also improving the passenger's comfort. The lesson for leaders is that while the CEO of a technology company does not need to be an engineer, he or she must be able to grasp how that technology will create value for customers.

HE SHIFTS RESOURCES TO PROJECTS WITH THE HIGHEST PROFIT POTENTIAL

To develop successful new products, companies need both capital and people. But many companies waste their capital and their people on unproductive programs. This is thanks in part to the mentality that researchers need unfettered resources in order to be creative and get a lucky break. But McNerney manages product development by balancing creativity and discipline. He encourages experimentation and creativity, but he targets his investments at the projects that appear to promise the biggest returns.

At 3M, he created a new process for allocating R&D resources. He shifted many scientists into 3M's business units and centralized the part of 3M's R&D organization that focused on breakthrough technologies. Moreover, he encouraged managers to shut down R&D projects that lacked the potential to create at least $100 million in revenues within a few quarters, so that the money could be allocated to projects with greater economic potential. While McNerney's approach to changing 3M's R&D culture met with significant resistance, 3M also increased its share of revenues from new products as a result.

When he became CEO of 3M, McNerney discovered that 3M was a company run on legends and an undisciplined culture of experimentation. He saw that he needed to alter the way 3M's R&D was motivated in order to encourage it to invest in projects with the most potential to add value to customers and 3M shareholders.

The 3M that McNerney inherited was sprawling and lacked strategic focus. 3M had 148 plants in sixty countries; 53 percent of sales were outside the United States. It had 1,500 products in development. Its organizational chart was confusing. Wall Street complained that its mix of faster-growing and more lethargic businesses made its performance and prospects difficult to evaluate. As Robert J. Burgstahler, former 3M chief financial officer, said, "The thing that always stuck in my mind was an investor's comment that 3M was a place where he'd love to work, but he just didn't know if he would invest in the company."[17]

One element of McNerney's response to this corporate lethargy was to restructure 3M's R&D operation. McNerney hoped this initiative would speed up the way 3M developed new products and brought them to customers. This "3M Acceleration" process was intended to change 3M's product development approach through the following initiatives:

- **Goal setting.** In January 2001, McNerney challenged 3M to achieve 5 percent to 8 percent annual growth from internally developed new products—which he called "organic growth." To accomplish this, McNerney wanted researchers to screen development projects moving through a stage-gate system

(SGS). Think of an SGS as a series of hurdles on a track that get taller and taller as a runner moves forward. The runner can only reach the finish line if she can leap over each of the hurdles in turn. If she can't make it over a hurdle, the race is over. Similarly, for development projects, a new technology must leap over a series of increasingly tall hurdles to reach the market. McNerney hoped that the SGS would **double** the number of new ideas leaping over the first such hurdle—known as the *beginning of commercialization*—and would **triple** the number of products hurdling the final one—*full-scale launch*. Although the primary goal was to increase the number of products reaching the market, it was also crucial to screen out the unsuccessful tries before much money had been spent. These seemingly contradictory goals were in fact mutually supporting. That's because if a failed attempt could be killed early, it would free up resources that could be spent on the products with the most commercial potential. McNerney dubbed this goal "2x/3x."[18]

- **Centralized technology development.** McNerney believed that too much of 3M's R&D budget was being spent on scientists in white coats conducting pure research into topics that were of great scientific interest to them, but not necessarily to anyone else. However, while some of their efforts might find their way into 3M products, many were difficult to commercialize. McNerney was not certain about how much of this pure research was valuable to 3M, but he thought it occupied too much overhead. When McNerney arrived at 3M, these researchers operated in twelve technology centers. To reduce the overhead associated with these centers, McNerney consolidated these scientists into one corporate research lab—bringing 3M's five hundred researchers under one organization divided into four sections: materials, pro-

cesses, software/electronics/mechanical systems, and analytical.[19]

- **Analysis of R&D projects.** McNerney encouraged researchers to analyze their projects—to assess such business variables as the project's potential commercial application, the
size of the market, and possible manufacturing concerns. Before McNerney's arrival, 3M did not analyze R&D projects; it
simply refreshed annual budgets based on how much money
they had the year before. 3M's hope then was that eventually
these projects would yield a successful new product. But Mc-
Nerney wanted 3M to take a more disciplined approach, so he
limited investment to projects with the potential to generate
at least $100 million in sales by creating significant value for
customers.[20]

- **Decentralized product development.** McNerney took hundreds of other 3M researchers out of the "ivory towers" and
moved them into 3M's business units. McNerney assigned
four hundred of 3M's technical people to its seven "market-
focused businesses." This required the researchers to work
with people with different functional skills. According to
Andrew Ouderkirk, a corporate scientist with the Display
and Graphics business, who led the development of 3M's mul-
tilayer optical films, "While we tend to focus on innovation
as coming up with the original idea, getting ideas to market
quickly in the form of useful customer products requires innovation from nearly every skill set at the company from
R&D to manufacturing, to sales/marketing, to purchasing
and the supply chain."[21]

McNerney's 3M Acceleration infused product development
with a tighter market and financial discipline through the following processes:

- **Real-world scrutiny.** As ideas move through gates of the SGS, 3M analyzed them using "real, win, worth" analysis. This tool asked three questions: "Is the opportunity real?" "Can we win at it?" and "Is it worth it?" These questions seem quite basic, but they were formerly not asked by 3M scientists.

- **Different classes of novelty.** In fast-moving electronics businesses such as Ouderkirk's optical film area, early-stage ideas were screened as "revolutionary," "evolutionary," or "overlooked." 3M applied a different strategic approach and held up specific financial expectations for each category.

- **Involving customers in product development.** 3M encouraged interaction with customers in a structured meeting format that specified the role of individuals in these meetings, what information should be collected, and how to act on it. This structure was critical because 3M scientists had not previously worked with customers during product development.

- **Learning from experience.** 3M also introduced a "won/lost" process to analyze past new-product successes and failures. "Won/lost" provided insight that researchers could use to increase their odds of success on current projects.[22]

While these practices helped focus 3M's researchers working within its business units, its centralized R&D organization pursued a different strategy that was intended to keep 3M broadly competitive in international markets. The strategy of 3M's centralized R&D organization rested on three elements:

- Investing in technical capabilities where the customers are—which is increasingly outside the United States
- Continuing to nurture 3M's entrepreneurship based on its

traditional 15 percent rule, which enables engineers to spend 15 percent of their time on projects that interest them
- Keeping pace with external sources of technology[23]

McNerney believed that 3M Acceleration produced stronger relationships with key customers and new insights into the real-world problems those customers face. The program began with 130 customer projects, and McNerney expected the number to triple in the ensuing years. In the second half of 2003, McNerney's program had accelerated 3M's organic growth rate, and its new-product pipeline held as much as $5 billion of annual sales by his estimate. Following McNerney's departure from 3M, his successor scaled back parts of the 3M Acceleration program. Some of 3M's highly tenured R&D staff complained that the program favored more predictable, incremental development over bigger, more important, open-ended, blue-sky research. Regardless of the ultimate outcome, McNerney praised what he called "a single, company-wide process for new product introductions," which he hoped would accelerate 3M's organic growth.[24]

McNerney's experiences suggest six lessons for leaders:

- Innovation and discipline are not mutually exclusive.
- Leaders must allow creative people significant freedom within a clear business framework.
- The business framework should stress the need to apply technologies to attractive markets where the company has the potential to gain enough market share to warrant the investment.
- The business framework should kill projects before too much money has been spent, so that projects with the greatest commercial potential will have sufficient resources.
- Leaders should retain a core of pure researchers but push

more of them into the business units so they can help commercialize their technical expertise.

- Leaders should encourage R&D to advance the state of the art
in technology and to operate globally.

CONCLUSION

Matching technology to the needs of customers is a critical skill
for the leader of a technology company. By doing that, McNerney
has introduced winning products that have contributed significantly to corporate revenues. He helped to push through the GE90,
which generated $25 billion in revenue potential for GE. As a Boe-
ing director and then CEO, he contributed to the introduction of
the 787, which has generated over nine hundred customer orders.
At the core of these successes is McNerney's ability to listen to the
needs of customers and to harness the engineering and other
product development skills needed to deliver products that meet
these customer needs in a competitively superior manner. But
McNerney also recognizes that despite the uncertain nature of
innovation, he can make product development more disciplined by
shifting capital and people from weak or irrelevant projects to
ones with strong potential.

CHAPTER 5.

INVEST IN YOUR STRENGTHS

When Jim McNerney took over as CEO at Boeing, he gave a speech in which he said, "Always pursue a strategy that your competitors can't copy."[1] In saying this, he articulated one of the most basic principles of strategy. If a competitor can copy what you're doing, then your company will not have a unique position on the competitive battlefield. To win customers, employees, capital, and high shareholder returns, CEOs must forge and execute strategies that competitors can't match. And while it's essential for a company to do something different, the strategy can't be different just for the sake of uniqueness. It has to help the company win in multiple competitive arenas.

An effective business strategy is a set of *internally consistent choices* about a firm's *goals* and the *means of achieving them* that *uniquely position* the company on the *business battlefield*. It's important for the choices to be internally consistent, because if they're not, then the company won't achieve the goals. For example, if a company chooses to be the low-cost producer, it needs to charge the lowest **prices** in the industry and pick functional policies—such as how to purchase its supplies and manufacture its products—that will give it the lowest **costs** in the industry.

Leaders initiate strategy by articulating goals, such as market share, revenue, and profit targets. Then leaders develop a plan for how the firm will achieve those goals by offering specific products, targeting particular market segments, and performing its business activities—such as purchasing, manufacturing, and sales—in a particular way. For example, Starbucks chose to become "a third place"—home and work being the other two—where people could spend time. To achieve this goal, Starbucks bought high-quality coffee beans and coffee preparation equipment, staffed its stores with personable, enthusiastic, well-compensated employees, and created a store environment that invited people to hang out with friends or work on their computers. The result was rapid global growth and much-higher-than-industry-average prices and margins.

When Starbucks first began its expansion, the uniqueness of its positioning was quite apparent compared to the other coffee shops and fast food chains with which it competed. But to succeed, Starbucks had to compete not only for scarce customers but also for talented employees and managers, high-quality raw materials, capital for expansion, and motivated investors.

To win customers, the company's product or service must satisfy customer requirements better than competitors'. To attract and retain the best employees and managers, a human resources strategy must create a more compelling work environment than competitors'. And to attract equity capital, the firm must exceed investors' expectations by a greater proportion and more reliably than competitors'. The CEO must formulate strategy and then manage the organization so that strategy gets translated into specific actions that lead to superior performance.

During his tenures at GE, 3M, and Boeing, McNerney has demonstrated the ability to create and execute such strategies. How does McNerney achieve this?

- He focuses on big, growing markets.
- He invests in existing strengths and tackles weaknesses.
- He analyzes and exploits competitor weaknesses.

HE FOCUSES ON BIG, GROWING MARKETS

Before he became Boeing's CEO, McNerney was a Boeing director, and in that role he helped develop the strategy that allowed Boeing to make the right bet on which group of customers would be most profitable. Boeing focused on the midsize planes needed by the point-to-point airline segment, while Airbus targeted the larger planes used by the long-range, hub segment. As it turned out, Boeing made the smarter bet.

How did McNerney know that Boeing should bet on the midsize market? He took a clear-eyed look at the potential customers and what they wanted. Unlike Airbus, which may have fallen victim to confirmation bias[2]—the tendency to see only data that reinforces a preexisting expectation—McNerney relied strongly on Boeing's Strategic Analysis Department (SAD).[3]

As an independent unit, SAD gathers data, analyzes it, and comes to a conclusion about the size of a market without pressure to slant the results to satisfy the demands of Boeing executives. SAD asks its Airline Advisory Council, consisting of Boeing's best customers, what they would like in a new aircraft. And it looks at trends in the airline industry—such as changing route structures and new business objectives (for example, an emphasis on profit versus market share).

As a board member, in 2001 McNerney supported the approval of what ultimately amounted to the $10 billion investment in the 787. The board agreed to the investment because it was convinced that the market was out there and that Boeing could succeed by building on its strengths. The evidence for the size of the market, interestingly enough, came both from Boeing's strategic analysts and from market research done jointly with its biggest rival, Airbus Industries.

In the mid-1990s, Boeing had been trying to decide what to do about its highly profitable 747 jumbo jet program, which was reaching the end of its life. Boeing was considering whether to develop a "growth version" of the 747, which would increase its capacity to 500 seats from 420 seats. But Boeing's profits were dwindling because demand for the 747 was falling off, and it was cutting production volume. Although Boeing had made enormous profits from the 747, it was not certain that there would be a sufficient market for such a large aircraft in the future.[4]

So Boeing proposed to Airbus that the two companies conduct a joint study to assess the market potential for a replacement version of the 747. Why Airbus agreed to this joint study is not clear. Some observers think that Airbus welcomed the opportunity to learn more about the market and the technology for jumbo aircraft. It may have also hoped that Boeing would spill the beans on useful information that would help Airbus build a bigger aircraft.[5]

Others contend that the joint research project on the next-generation 747 might have been a deliberate Boeing tactic to stall Airbus and to get it to divert resources that might have been more profitably invested.[6] Richard Aboulafia, vice president of Teal Group, an aerospace consulting firm, and others think that Airbus—which lacked a jumbo aircraft—had fuselage envy. As Aboulafia puts it, Airbus exhibited "hubris. They told themselves, 'If we have the biggest plane, we will beat Boeing.' "[7]

In any event, at the end of the joint study, Boeing concluded that the superjumbo market would be far smaller than Airbus did. According to John Walsh of Walsh Aviation, an aerospace consulting firm, Boeing estimated that demand for superjumbo aircraft would amount to 250 units, while Airbus thought the market would total 1,000.[8] Like Airbus, Boeing believed that size matters, but it wasn't the size of the plane that Boeing wanted to maximize. It was the size of the market and Boeing's potential share of it that mattered. At McNerney's urging, Boeing remained focused on the market for intermediate-sized jets, which proved to be the better bet.

HE INVESTS IN EXISTING STRENGTHS AND TACKLES WEAKNESSES

In selecting which markets to pursue and setting the strategy for pursuing them, McNerney carefully assesses his own company's strengths and weaknesses. While the market for the midsize 787 might be substantial, it would not make sense for Boeing to pursue it if it couldn't profitably sell and deliver enough units to justify the investment of its capital.

Building on his experience selling engines to Boeing and Airbus while at GE, McNerney had a good understanding of the critical activities needed to compete. And he decided to invest in the critical activities where Boeing was strong and outsource the rest. In McNerney's view, Boeing's core competencies included "design, engineering, [and] systems integration." For the other activities, such as making "higher-level components," McNerney found "high-level partners."[9]

When he started, McNerney admitted that he was not sure to what extent Boeing should design and make some of these components itself and how much to outsource to suppliers. As he put it, "How far would we go? I'm not sure. We're going to learn from the 787 experience. The designer has to build a certain part of the plane, too. So we're going to feel our way on exactly how much we can delegate to our partners and how much we can't. We don't have any specific goal. We're just trying to get the 787 done and learn from it. One foot in front of the other. We have no grand plan."[10]

But McNerney's modesty masks the pressure he puts on Boeing to get better. While it has clear competitive strengths—particularly in design and support—Boeing has opportunities to improve in systems integration and assembly. Though the delay in delivering the 787 is disappointing to Boeing's customers and clearly demonstrates its need to improve, McNerney's efforts to confront and overcome Boeing's problems are likely to make Boeing a stronger competitor.

In relation to Airbus, Boeing has many competitive advantages. It outperforms its competitor in a number of areas, but McNerney isn't satisfied just to look at Boeing's abilities versus Airbus's. He looks up and down the chain of potential suppliers, and if he sees that someone else can do a job better than Boeing, he will outsource the job so that Boeing can focus on doing what it does best and deliver the best product to customers.

The ability to freely outsource is a big competitive strength for Boeing. While Boeing can use international suppliers who are the best in their particular category of technology, Airbus, because of its government ownership, is forced to hire engineers who reside in the European countries where Airbus operates. These countries are not necessarily the technology leaders in all categories.

Another Boeing advantage is that it uses a single computer-aided design (CAD) system for designing commercial aircraft—ironically enough—from the French company Dassault. By contrast, Airbus used two systems—a German one and a French one. The two systems could not work together, which resulted in a flawed design for the A380. Airbus had to build the first twenty-five A380 aircraft by hand to fix the resulting problems.[11] Boeing's use of a single CAD system enabled it to work with its component supplier more efficiently than did Airbus. That's because Boeing and its suppliers used a single common database for all the aircraft designs. Since Airbus had two separate databases, it needed to reconcile differences that emerged between them in order to complete the design work. While it's likely that Airbus will itself try to move to a single database—potentially erasing Boeing's advantage—during the development of the 787, Airbus's dual database put Boeing at a competitive advantage due to the extra time Airbus took to reconcile the two databases.

And Boeing has been able to protect much of the new technology that it's developed for the 787. Through a combination of patents and contractual arrangements with suppliers, Boeing has made it very difficult for Airbus to discover and copy Boeing's technological innovations. Not only do these legal tactics help protect Boeing's technology, but the sheer magnitude of Boeing's revenues creates a powerful financial incentive for Boeing's suppliers to keep its technology under wraps. Boeing has made it clear that if a supplier leaks its technology, Boeing will investigate the leak and cut off those responsible from future business.[12] As a result, if Boeing invests in an innovative technology, it is likely to be able to recoup its investment without worrying about Airbus copying it. The result is a quicker payback period for Boeing's technological innovation than it would enjoy if it had to share the potential profits with Airbus's knockoffs.

In systems integration and assembly, Boeing is also better than Airbus; however, they both have problems. *Systems integration* means pulling together all the diverse engineering subsystems of an aircraft so the entire system works together seamlessly. For example, the 787 has ninety-two distinct subsystems—all of which must work together effectively if the 787 is to fly safely. Two such subsystems are avionics—which controls the wing surfaces—and radar. In one airplane program, Boeing's Wedgetail,

a 737 modified for surveillance purposes, the radar system designed by Northrop Grumman overpowered the avionics system.
Both needed to be redesigned as a result. *Assembly* refers to the
snapping together of the components—Boeing hopes to be able to
do this in three days once its 787 program is working well.[13]

Despite the problems, McNerney is committed to using Boeing's strength in systems integration and assembly for future
Boeing aircraft. As we'll see in chapter 9, McNerney has worked
out many of the problems with the outsourcing strategy. As a
result, Boeing will reap its benefits, which include lower capital
costs, access to best-in-class suppliers, and quicker time to
market.

Boeing also outperforms Airbus when it comes to support—
which includes selling spare parts and providing information for
pilot navigation. As we'll explore in chapter 6, McNerney has invested significantly in enhancing this Boeing strength. In May
2006, Boeing spent $1.7 billion on aviation parts distributor Aviall.
Boeing bought the industry's biggest independent provider of new
aviation parts and services so it could accelerate its growth in a
$25 billion industry where it was already a major competitor. Sup-
port is a significant source of profit because it continues for years
after an aircraft is delivered and it requires a relatively small capital investment. Boeing does a better job of support, in part because, unlike Airbus, it is not saddled with the European labor
union requirement that support workers be kept on the payroll
whether or not there is demand for their services. Boeing can ad-
just its work force to the amount of work. Thus, it can keep its
costs more in line with customer demand and operate more profitably.[14]

Boeing has decided that manufacturing aircraft from
scratch—rather than assembling components made by others—is
a weakness, and it has taken steps to shed manufacturing facili-

ties. While it has encountered resistance from unions in its efforts to sell these facilities, these unions are far less powerful than the ones in Europe. Boeing has sold manufacturing operations in Wichita, Kansas, and St. Louis, Missouri, and in both instances faced far less resistance than Airbus faces when it tries to close or sell plants. In exchange for its government subsidies, Airbus has sacrificed a great deal of flexibility to reduce the size of its work force.[15]

Boeing currently enjoys a temporary advantage over Airbus thanks to the weak dollar. That's because Boeing sells aircraft in dollars and pays suppliers and many employees in dollars. The weakness in the dollar makes its aircraft prices more attractive to non-U.S. customers who have stronger currencies. However, the bigger advantage over Airbus is that Airbus sells in dollars but pays suppliers and employees in higher-valued euros. The result is that Airbus's profits are squeezed while Boeing enjoys wider margins. However, this advantage could evaporate if the dollar strengthens relative to the euro.[16] For the time being, the weak dollar enables Boeing to offer lower prices to customers in those markets—such as Europe and Asia—where the local currencies are stronger than the dollar. This advantage over Airbus is particularly pronounced in Europe, because Airbus pays its employees in euros and sells its aircraft in lower-valued dollars, thus squeezing its margins.

Finally, Boeing has a less tangible but still significant advantage over Airbus—the discipline of public equity markets. EADS, Airbus's parent company, is a public holding company; however, only a third of its shares are publicly traded. The other two thirds are held by European governments. Airbus may have rushed through the investment in the A380 because its executives knew that EADS would be born—and that the public scrutiny would make it harder to justify the A380 investment. Even with EADS in place, Boeing must respond much more quickly than Airbus to public stockholders. While this shareholder scrutiny can be painful in the short run, over the longer term it gives Boeing an advantage over Airbus because it makes it hard for Boeing to make any A380-scale investment blunders.[17] The public-company advantage forces McNerney to anticipate problems and solve them much more quickly than Airbus, which can get away with a more lethargic approach thanks to its more coddled ownership status.

All of these factors allowed McNerney to make the case that Boeing not only was targeting a large market, but also could perform the activities—either internally or with partners—it needed to gain a significant share of that market. Boeing was strong in design, systems integration, assembly, and support. And in the design and manufacture of components, Boeing had relationships with world-class partners to tackle its weaknesses there. Boeing struggled with its production schedule, but McNerney learned important lessons that will enable Boeing to apply its strengths to future product generations.

HE ANALYZES AND EXPLOITS
COMPETITOR WEAKNESSES

To persuade Boeing's board to go forward with the 787, McNerney needed one more piece of the puzzle. He needed to show that if Boeing made the 787 investment, Airbus wouldn't cut too deeply into its profits. After all, even though the midrange market was big—roughly three thousand aircraft—and Boeing had (or could partner to get) the skills it needed to build the 787, if Boeing had to fight Airbus for every order, its share of the market might not be big enough to provide shareholders an attractive return on investment.

But McNerney argued that Boeing would have a big head

start on Airbus. Based on his knowledge of Airbus and Boeing, gained from selling aircraft engines to both while at GE, McNerney knew Airbus would not be able to copy the 787 very quickly.

That was for two reasons. The first was that Airbus was a complex multinational organization that was rife with internal conflicts. Its mission was to employ European workers—profit was of secondary importance. And in trying to make decisions, the UK branch of Airbus was often at odds with the Spanish, French, and German ones. The second was Airbus's decision, which was influenced by these internal conflicts, to invest in the superjumbo A380 because it thought that this aircraft would deal a coup de grâce to Boeing. Airbus's decision diverted resources to the relatively small superjumbo market. McNerney saw that this would help Boeing because it meant that Airbus did not have the capital available to invest in a midsize craft.

Boeing has been able to exploit the inherent weaknesses in Airbus's corporate mission and ownership structure. EADS, which until 2006[18] owned 80 percent of Airbus's shares along with Britain's BAE Systems, has a significant challenge coordinating the operations of four companies representing different European nations; they have a long history with one another and political goals that may be at odds with one another. According to Pierre Dussauge, a professor at HEC, a French business school, "The main disadvantage of Airbus is that it continues to be four companies merged into one, and they are working independently." These four companies include France's Aérospatiale, Germany's Deutsche Aerospace, Spain's Construcciones Aeronáuticas Sociedad Anónima (CASA), and the UK's British Aerospace. In the struggle to keep each of these companies happy, EADS can't create an efficient global network of suppliers.[19] That's because the world's best supplier of, say, a fuselage, might be in Japan, but since none of EADS's member companies are Japanese, it would have to try to find a fuselage supplier within France, Spain, Germany, or the UK so it could employ citizens of those countries.

Boeing lost market share to Airbus in the 1990s because it underestimated Airbus as a competitive threat and did not respond to its new products aggressively enough. Boeing's loss of market share and the resulting financial impact forced it to take risks and rethink its business strategy while Airbus continued its old ways of operating. In Dussauge's view, Boeing's response to the stress of being beaten by Airbus caused it to become "much more integrated." Further, after losing its supremacy, "it was obliged to take more risks and innovate more." A similar process had happened at Airbus during the 1980s, and it paid off for Airbus with its resulting leadership position in the 1990s. At the time, "Boeing was dominant and did not innovate much, while Airbus introduced most of the innovations in this sector."[20] Nevertheless, Airbus felt inferior because Boeing still built the 747, the largest aircraft in the market.

Airbus's envy was not the only reason it overestimated the size of the market. Thanks to the dominance on Boeing's board of reluctant-to-invest McDonnell Douglas executives, Airbus assumed that Boeing would not dare to offer a competing aircraft because that would require so much additional capital. Airbus assumed that Boeing would decline to invest in any new aircraft, as McDonnell Douglas had. Simply put, Airbus thought the A380 would be the final nail in Boeing's coffin.[21]

While Airbus thought it was delivering the coup de grâce to Boeing, Boeing thought it was getting the better of Airbus and that it would take Airbus a long time to figure that out and to respond. Specifically, Boeing believed that Airbus's internal conflicts would slow down its response to Boeing's success with the 787 in the midrange market. As it turned out, the A380 exacerbated those conflicts. British members of Airbus agreed with Boeing's more conservative market forecast for the superjumbo. While the French contingent was inclined toward the much higher estimate for A380 sales, Airbus's German subsidiary was somewhere between the large and small estimates.

According to aerospace financial consultant Phillip Bolt, who worked on the forecast while at former UK-based Airbus partner BAE Systems, "We hewed to the view that the market for the smaller, three-hundred-seat aircraft would be bigger and more profitable than that for the large aircraft. However, the Franco-German momentum overwhelmed BAE's view. And BAE exited from its Airbus shareholdings at the appropriate moment. I don't think the A380 will ever be profitable without the soft loans and government subsidies."[22]

Airbus's decision to go forward with the A380 delayed its ability to respond to the market demand for the 787. According to a European industry insider who agreed to speak frankly on condition of anonymity, "Boeing knew that the market for a growth 747 sold to the passenger airline industry would be limited. There might be demand for a military version, and possibly a Japanese carrier would be interested. But Airbus's decision to invest in the A380 meant it had no money to build an aircraft to compete with the 787."[23]

Airbus ended up spending at least $12 billion on the A380. This "catastrophic diversion of resources" was an enormous self-inflicted wound that is now starving Airbus for resources as it tries to catch up with Boeing's 787. Not only did Airbus invest significantly in the A380, but it grossly overestimated the market size. Therefore, it is unlikely that Airbus will sell enough A380s to break even. Between December 2000 and May 2008, Airbus sold a total of 192 A380s—and most of those to a single customer. That indicates that the market is roughly 80 percent smaller than Airbus had anticipated. But Aboulafia credits McNerney with the key strategic decision that put Boeing in such an advantageous position vis-à-vis Airbus. He believes that if McNerney had not pushed Boeing to invest in the 787, Airbus might have realized its ambition of dealing a lethal blow to Boeing.[24]

As suggested above, Airbus eventually did wake up and realize that it needed to compete with Boeing in the midrange market. But the 787 is "more innovative" than the A350, which is Airbus's midrange offering. Meanwhile, according to Boeing, the A350 "makes obsolete" the A330 and A340—which have between 240 and 320 seats. Yet the A350 has had a cool reception from the airlines, with orders running at a pace that is only one third that of the Boeing 787. In addition, the A350 is going to be remodeled because of criticism from several customers. Airbus's declining credibility vis-à-vis Boeing became more evident in 2006 when Singapore Airlines chose to order twenty Boeing 787s.[25]

Not only does Boeing have an innovation advantage over Airbus, but, despite Boeing's 787 delivery challenges, it also has a scheduling advantage over the A350. The 787 is a radically new technology involving a tubular all-composite fuselage. By contrast, the A350 design is not unique. It is an improvement on an old design. But even with the A350's less ambitious technology, it is expected to be delayed until 2013 at the earliest. By contrast, the 787 looks to be delayed roughly eighteen months—until late 2009.[26]

McNerney sums up Boeing's assessment of the superjumbo market quite succinctly. As he says, "On the A380, we never felt that the market was that big, we felt it was a niche market and with huge development costs. We could never make the business case work for that huge airplane. Instead we focused on smaller, fuel-efficient 777s and 787s. It was pure business analysis."[27]

With his *pure business analysis*, McNerney helped push Boeing's board to unlock the capital needed to go after a large, growing market in which it had a competitive advantage over Airbus. And in so doing, he revealed four lessons for leaders:

- Encourage objective analysis and debate to keep confirmation bias out of estimates.
- Choose large, growing markets over small ones that may not grow enough to support the new product's investment.
- Make sure you have—or can partner to obtain—the skills needed to win a big share of that market.
- Analyze competitors' goals, strategies, and capabilities to assess whether your company can win enough market share to earn back the investment.

CONCLUSION

McNerney has built on Boeing's strengths to help it win a substantial amount of new business. Despite problems delivering the 787, Boeing has cleverly exploited Airbus's weaknesses. It targeted the midrange market while Airbus was distracted by its focus on the smaller jumbo segment. This strategy turned an $8 billion investment in a midrange, fuel-efficient aircraft into 896 orders.[28] Moreover, because it chose to pursue a long-range jumbo jet, Airbus found itself chasing Boeing in this market with a product that lacked innovative technology and was likely to be introduced to the market no earlier than 2013—many years after Boeing's current target delivery date of late 2009. By building on its strengths, Boeing has prevailed over Airbus.

CHAPTER 6.

GROW THROUGH PEOPLE, NOT DEALS

Achieving profitable growth is one of the most important responsibilities of a CEO. Profitable growth depends both on generating higher revenues and on keeping costs as low as practical so that more of those higher revenues flow to the bottom line.

Basically, a CEO can get this growth from two sources: new products that the company develops itself, or acquisition of companies. At both 3M and Boeing, McNerney has made it clear that he prefers the internal growth model. At a retreat for top executives in Orlando, Florida, soon after he joined Boeing, one of the first topics on McNerney's agenda, according to an insider at the meeting, was to declare that he expected the company to grow "organically"—rather than by acquisition.[1]

Before McNerney joined Boeing, the company had made a series of acquisitions, including McDonnell Douglas in 1997 and Hughes Satellite in 2000. When McNerney became CEO in 2005, these businesses still were not completely integrated. Instead, they pursued their own independent interests rather than those of a unified Boeing. One reason McNerney resists growth through acquisitions is that it's hard to merge the cultures and operations of acquired companies.

Another reason McNerney says he is reluctant to make acquisitions is that they relieve a company of the obligation to chart its own destiny. Also, he believes that investment bankers have too large a role in shaping deals, and the prices are often too high. Unless a company is eager to sell, purchase prices tend to capitalize future profit growth. This makes the prices on most deals so high that acquirers can't earn back the premium they pay to make the acquisition in the first place.

McNerney's choice of strategy for organic growth depends on the company and the industry it is in. For example, at 3M the challenge was to focus thousands of research projects and increase the odds that they would lead to new products that customers would buy. By contrast, at Boeing, each individual new product could cost billions of dollars—an investment that is hardly guaranteed to earn back its cost. So while at 3M McNerney needed to develop multiple smaller products, at Boeing the challenge remains to succeed with fewer bet-the-company investments a decade.

To generate organic growth, McNerney does the following:

- He holds people accountable for growth.
- He applies current strengths to new markets.
- He makes acquisitions that complement organic growth.

HE HOLDS PEOPLE ACCOUNTABLE FOR GROWTH

To encourage organic growth, the first thing McNerney does is to get people in the company to take responsibility for growth. He promotes his view that acquisitions are a cop-out for companies that can't develop new products and services on their own. And he leaves no room for business units to wiggle out of responsibility for generating new products themselves.

A few months before departing 3M for Boeing, McNerney

gave a speech at MIT about how 3M grows organically. McNerney's key point was that 3M's ability to survive for one hundred years was due largely to its organic growth. As McNerney said in the speech, "Organic growth . . . the ability to reinvent itself from within," rather than by mergers and acquisitions, differentiated 3M from other hundred-year-old companies. However, when McNerney joined 3M in 2001, he said, he believed that its growth culture had become "stale."[2]

To revive it, McNerney's leadership team regrouped 3M's engineers into "results-focused, energized teams" while maintaining 3M's "creative and entrepreneurial spirit." As we discussed in chapter 4, McNerney developed a new product development strategy, 3M Acceleration, which separated the big-concept scientific research from the applied, product-focused research and used distinct ways of measuring each. In McNerney's view, this approach was the best of both worlds—it retained the creative freedom of the research and design teams while challenging the production teams to focus on generating sales and profits.[3]

McNerney believes that a CEO's power to get results comes from communicating his expectations and knowing that ambitious people will strive to meet those expectations. Or as McNerney puts it, "How do you get organic growth? You expect it." This expectation put an edge into 3M's "Minnesota nice" culture by focusing it on meeting externally oriented goals, such as higher revenue growth and increased market share, rather than on internal measures, such as ensuring that all business lines got an equal share of corporate resources.[4]

McNerney reorganized 3M's divisions around *markets*—such as health care and transportation—rather than around *product groups* such as tapes, abrasives, and adhesives, as it had been organized previously.[5] This shift from a product to a market structure pushed 3M to change from a company focused inwardly to one that faced outward toward customers and competitors. Focusing 3M on markets allowed McNerney to hold the newly market-focused division managers accountable for growth.

Because 3M had forty-five divisions, some too small to justify having their own manufacturing, research, and other facilities under their complete control, this reorganization created a structure that was a bit more complex than might be ideal. To achieve needed efficiencies, McNerney required the smaller divisions to *share resources* in a structure it called a *global matrix*. "We have the legitimate need for a global matrix," he said, "and knowing how to manage it is critically important. We're approaching [being] a $20 billion company. [But] we have 45 divisions, which is a lot of divisions for a company that size, and many of them really aren't big enough to carry their own global operations, so they have to share. It's the way we capture scale the best way we know how."[6]

Despite 3M's complexity, McNerney's efforts to focus it externally drove division managers to think more about how well they met the needs of customers in those markets, rather than focusing simply on how much their product revenue had increased from the year before. By pressing division managers to think about how 3M created value for customers, McNerney encouraged them to create new products and services that would help capture a bigger share of the customer's budget and deliver faster organic growth at 3M.[7]

At 3M, McNerney was fortunate to inherit a growth-oriented culture, albeit one that was a bit inward-looking and stagnated. He didn't have to create a hunger for creativity in 3M workers; he simply had to make them more productive. To achieve that, McNerney tweaked 3M's culture by focusing its undisciplined and self-fulfillment-oriented spirit onto external markets. It wasn't that 3Mers had not focused on growth in the past; it was just that each researcher believed that his or her idea would be the next Post-it note. McNerney tried to channel this creative spirit in a way that would result in more new products that actually made it to the market. McNerney said that he had inherited "a legacy where everybody wakes up in the morning trying to figure out how to grow the company. Some of the ideas are pretty wacky, but better to try to herd the cats than have no cats at all."[8]

At Boeing, McNerney also expects growth from its people. Seeking to eliminate the idea that acquisitions would relieve Boeing of the responsibility to grow internally, McNerney told a reporter in 2006: "We play in big markets. We have tremendous capability in this company, and I want us to all depend on each other for growth. I don't want people in our company to have the feeling that I'm going to replace the inability to grow ourselves with buying things. CEOs can do that," but then people in the organization start wondering, " 'Is he depending on me or is he depending on Goldman Sachs or Morgan Stanley to grow the place?' I want us to depend on each other, which doesn't mean that we're not going to do acquisitions to accelerate our organic capability."[9]

As he did at 3M, McNerney stresses the central importance of organic growth at Boeing. "Our model for growth is time-tested," he says, "We are driving growth primarily from organic—or internal—sources. We are well positioned in healthy, growing markets, with industry-leading products and services. And we need to take full advantage of this position to capture more market share and further grow our quarter-trillion-dollar backlog."[10]

While growth is a responsibility that McNerney wants everyone at Boeing to share, he institutionalized the importance of growth by creating the position of vice president of new development and strategy. In March 2006, McNerney appointed Shephard Hill to the newly created post overseeing Boeing's business development and strategy. Hill joined Boeing's Executive Council and reports directly to McNerney. His responsibilities include analyzing and developing plans to "drive Boeing's growth" and "nurturing developing businesses." As McNerney says, Boeing's long-term growth plans require "a leader who is focused solely on our forward-looking efforts. [Hill] shapes the company's growth by ensuring that we approach it as a disciplined process that is fully integrated with our overall strategic direction."[11]

McNerney also reorganized Boeing's Integrated Defense Systems unit to spur growth. Specifically, he reduced the number of IDS business units from seven to three. This reorganization reduced Boeing's costs in response to an expected slowdown in Pentagon spending. The new units also help IDS to sell to the Pentagon, which has changed its focus from a defense policy aimed at creating a bigger nuclear arsenal than the Soviet Union to one intended to protect against unpredictable terrorist attacks. The Pentagon calls its new approach "capabilities-based" defense. In response, Boeing organized its three new IDS profit centers around three sets of capabilities: precision engagement and mobility systems, support systems and networks, and space systems. McNerney also believes that Boeing needs to be more efficient in order to compete for shrinking defense budgets. As he has said, "The units in IDS are set up to have stronger functional discipline and focus on execution, because that becomes even more important in a moderating environment."[12]

McNerney has placed the onus for growth on the people at 3M and Boeing. The techniques he has used suggest four lessons for leaders:

- Create a growth culture by setting clear expectations of higher growth.
- Reinforce the growth culture by organizing divisions around customer groups rather than products.

- Measure these divisions based on market share and growth goals.
- Consider creating an executive position charged with spurring corporate growth and strategic direction.

HE APPLIES CURRENT STRENGTHS
TO NEW MARKETS

McNerney knows well that simply holding people *accountable* for growth will not automatically lead people to *achieve* that growth. Holding people accountable certainly makes them want to achieve growth. However, in order to get the desired results, people must have the right resources and focus them on the right groups of customers. McNerney has demonstrated at 3M and Boeing that growth comes from applying a company's current strengths to new markets.

For example, from the beginning of 2001, when he joined 3M, until the third quarter of 2003, McNerney achieved seven consecutive quarters of record sales. 3M's growth under McNerney during this period is particularly significant because it happened during a period of very tepid growth in the United States. In the third quarter of 2003, worldwide sales, including brands such as Post-it and Scotch-Brite, totaled $4.616 billion, the third consecutive quarter of record sales and an increase of 11.4 percent from the third quarter of 2002.[13]

That revenue growth also boosted profits. 3M's net income for the third quarter of 2003 was $633 million, or $0.83 per share, up over 20 percent from the $545 million, or $0.69 a share, in the third quarter of 2002.[14] And for the full year, earnings before special items posted a 21 percent rise to $3.07 a share.[15]

How did McNerney achieve this outcome at 3M? He took two approaches:

- **Use a global organization to sell existing products to developing markets.** Developing markets are growing far more rapidly than Western markets. For instance, China and India have experienced gross domestic product growth averaging roughly 10 percent for much of the last decade, whereas U.S. GDP growth is at a virtual standstill at best. As these countries grow, they construct buildings, highways, and utilities. This growth creates opportunities for U.S. suppliers, especially at a time when a weak dollar makes their high-quality products a good value to customers. And given the relatively slow demand growth in Western markets, if a company like 3M expects to grow, it needs to gain share in those developing markets. Under McNerney's leadership, 3M used its international organization to achieve those market-share goals.
- **Refocus organization from products to customers.** Soon after he became CEO, McNerney concluded that 3M's organizational structure impeded its growth. That's because it was organized around products. McNerney believed that the product structure caused division managers to focus more on how they could boost sales of their current product lines than on working with customers to understand their changing needs and offering new products to satisfy those needs. To boost 3M's growth, McNerney changed 3M's organization from a product to a customer focus.

Use a Global Organization to Sell Existing Products to Developing Markets

McNerney saw 3M's global operations as a source of sustainable and profitable revenue growth. While he initially thought the structure might be too cumbersome, after leading 3M for several years he concluded that the structure worked well. 3M started operating globally at least seventy years ago, and it has survived through an effective combination of *local sensitivity* and *global scale*. 3M responds to country-specific market needs by forming *local partnerships* and by appointing *local employees* as general managers. The local sensitivity opens up relationships with distribution channels and end users. It also helps overcome regulatory and other barriers to generating revenues. The *global scale* provided the capital for McNerney to invest in specific countries where he perceived the most attractive growth opportunities for 3M.

When he took over as CEO in 2001, McNerney inherited a 3M that had operations in sixty countries and did business in two hundred countries through partnerships. As McNerney said, "We're very fortunate to have one of the strongest international organizations out there. We have been overseas for 50, 60, 70 years in some cases. Organizations have grown up [and] are run by locals, not run by U.S. people. We can get innovation out there from any country to all other countries faster than most."[16]

One existing product that 3M markets overseas is its composite conductors, which can transmit more power than conventional overhead power lines. As developing countries, such as China, build their infrastructure—including power lines—3M expects overseas demand for its composite conductors to grow.

Such sales of existing products to new markets helped boost 3M's earnings. For example, in 2005 McNerney extended 3M's forecast for 12 percent to 14 percent earnings per share (EPS) growth into 2006. McNerney told investors at a 3M meeting in New York, "One of the reasons our growth rate is accelerating is that we are doing disproportionately well in the developing economies. [Our international business is] our biggest growth platform."[17]

In 2004, 3M's business in emerging markets increased 23 percent in local currencies and accounted for $4 billion in sales, or almost a quarter of its total. McNerney expected that share to rise, because, as he put it, "There is an unusually strong match between the stuff we make and growing GDP rates and growing per-capita income. We often fly under the radar in places like China. All these things can be bought and sold without government intervention, by and large."[18] In 2004, 3M saw 29 percent sales growth in the China region in local currency, 14 percent in Brazil, and 18 percent in Eastern Europe. As McNerney pointed out, "[3M's products fit] very nicely with the rising aspirations of a middle class."[19]

McNerney has used 3M's global scale to tap into the exceptionally high growth in China and other parts of Asia. He invested 3M's capital and used its political connections to build logistics networks and overcome political obstacles in these Asian countries so that 3M's existing products could make their way to these developing markets. As McNerney said, "Yes, I think operating in Asia has its challenges logistically, politically. But, again, there is no choice for a diversified company like ours but to be there and to be aggressive. I would point to mainland China as a market that has always held huge promise. Add to that Korea, Taiwan, and there are mega growth opportunities out there, and we're aggressively deploying people and assets in all parts of those regions, and we're beginning to get paid back with very high double-digit growth."[20]

Refocus the Organization from Products to Customers

The ultimate form of organic growth is creating and selling new products that satisfy an unmet customer need. These products are riskier because of the significant investment required to bring them to market and the uncertainty about whether customers will buy them in sufficient numbers to pay a return on the investment. McNerney encouraged 3M to create such products by reorienting its divisions from a product focus to a customer focus. He did this to open the eyes of 3M's managers to the possibility that changing customer needs, new technologies, and upstart competitors required them to pursue new strategies for success.

McNerney inherited a 3M that was organized around both products and customer groups—and he changed it to one that focused on markets. His purpose was "to promote faster growth and a closer focus on [3M's] markets and customers." McNerney's reorganization created seven business units.[21] Three of the units were new, combining some inherited product-focused divisions into new customer-focused ones. Four of the divisions were left intact because they already targeted specific industry groups.[22]

One of the new units was the Transportation Business unit. McNerney's idea was to create a business unit that would sell existing and new products to manufacturers of transportation equipment, including automobiles, aircraft, and boats. McNerney combined into this unit products used in "the manufacture, repair and maintenance of automotive, marine, aircraft and other specialty vehicles." The products from 3M's old organization included components for catalytic converters, graphics, corrosion- and abrasion-resistant films, and masking tapes, to name a few.[23] McNerney's goal was to get 3M's Transportation Business more focused on boosting revenues from transportation companies. When he announced the establishment of the division in 2002, he explained, "These structural changes—driven by our strategic planning process—represent an important step toward better access to bigger, faster growing markets."[24]

At the annual meeting in 2004, he told shareholders: "In 2004, we're rededicating ourselves to hearing and valuing the voice of our customers as never before. We are increasingly viewed not just as product sellers, but as problem solvers—as a source of innovative solutions and a contributor to our customers' success. New products are the engine of 3M growth—always have been and always will be."[25]

McNerney has boosted Boeing's growth by applying its current strengths to new markets in three ways:

- **Exporting to developing countries.** As he did at 3M, McNerney has encouraged Boeing to sell its products to rapidly growing developing countries that are eager to purchase them.
- **Applying commercial technologies to defense markets.** McNerney has accelerated Boeing's growth by tailoring aircraft built for commercial markets so they will be valuable to defense industry customers.
- **Cooperating across Boeing to gain share in emerging markets.** McNerney encourages Boeing's commercial and defense sides to work together as they attack emerging markets. Traditionally, Boeing's two divisions have operated independently of one another. But McNerney is hoping that the cooperative approach will help establish a longer-term presence and create an advantage over new competitors as markets grow.

The evidence suggests that McNerney's growth strategies are working. As McNerney reported, "2007 revenues rose 8 percent to an all-time high of $66.4 billion, and our core earnings were up 35 percent. For the first time ever, our two big businesses—BCA and Boeing IDS—simultaneously achieved double-digit operating margins. Gains in productivity and performance in existing programs contributed significantly to earnings and helped offset additional investment in key growth programs."[26]

The company also built up a record backlog. Recapping 2007, McNerney said, "We also had our best year ever in capturing new business adding another $77 billion to a backlog that today totals $346 billion—more than five times our total revenues. Commercial Airplanes landed a record 1,423 airplane orders in 2007, reaching more than 1,000 orders for an unprecedented third consecutive year. Meanwhile, IDS won nine out of 11 strategically important competitions—an outstanding success rate, by any measure."[27]

Export to Developing Countries

McNerney pushed Boeing's commercial sales force to focus on the largest, most rapidly growing commercial aircraft markets in the world. In McNerney's judgment, those markets are in two regions of the world: Asia, which is growing thanks to its trade surplus with the United States, and the Middle East, which has generated enormous wealth reserves thanks to record oil prices. Boeing's push into these large, rapidly growing markets has contributed significantly to its growth.

At the 2008 annual meeting, McNerney reported: "Nearly 70 percent of our commercial backlog (as measured by revenue) is in high-value twin-aisle airplanes. It is spread across the world's leading airlines, which operate a wide variety of business models ranging from low-fare to full-service, short haul to long haul. Geographically speaking, only 11 percent of this backlog is with airlines based in the United States, where the current economic situation is a bit tenuous. A large part of our backlog is with customers in Asia and the Middle East, where economic conditions are more favorable."[28]

Boeing also obtained a significant amount of the growth in its **defense business** by selling existing products initially developed for U.S. defense customers to overseas ones. "That defense backlog is a healthy mix of both new and mature production and development programs that we believe we can continue to expand even through a period of more modest growth in U.S. defense spending," McNerney told shareholders. "In addition, we see significant potential in overseas defense markets." He continued by detailing significant sales in the UK, Australia, Japan, and Korea.[29]

Apply Commercial Technologies to Defense Markets

One of Boeing's unique sources of growth has been the use of its strengths in commercial aircraft to earn a significant share of military aircraft markets. Military customers in the United States and in international markets are eager to purchase Boeing aircraft that airlines have flown successfully. It takes only a relatively small investment for Boeing to modify existing commercial models to meet the needs of the military. Then it recoups that investment rather quickly as it delivers the aircraft to its military customers.

Since Boeing is strong in both commercial and military markets, it can profit from this process more than its competitors. As McNerney says, "We continue to see a distinct competitive advantage in being able to deliver commercial-derivative aircraft to our military customers both at home and abroad. The Airborne Laser for the U.S. Air Force is one example of that, where we are using a modified Boeing 747-400F. We also see potential for international versions of the P-8A Poseidon (based on the Next-Generation 737), which we are producing as a surveillance and anti-submarine aircraft for the U.S. Navy. And we are developing the 737-700 Airborne Early Warning and Control System for Australia, Turkey and Korea."[30]

Cooperate Across Boeing to Gain Share
in Emerging Markets

McNerney urges the divisions across Boeing to work together in search of international growth. He encourages cooperation, especially in markets that are rapidly industrializing and growing fast. Going after commercial and defense customers simultaneously helps Boeing gain share because it simplifies the shopping process for the customers. If a country can purchase aircraft and defense technology from a single firm, its contracting costs decline. McNerney believes Boeing will grow more rapidly when it presents a single face to these customers. In addition, in some countries with strong intellectual capital, Boeing can strengthen its ties by simultaneously selling products and buying services from local engineering companies.

Boeing has pursued this approach in India. As McNerney explains, "India [is] an example of how we are capitalizing on cooperation across our company to find new opportunities for growth internationally. With air travel in India growing at a phenomenal 25-percent annual rate, we are in the fortunate position of being the leading supplier of commercial airplanes to Indian carriers. We are also helping India to build its aviation infrastructure. We are buying from local Indian companies, and tapping into an amazing talent pool in engineering and technology. These companies, and others, could play an increasingly valuable role in driving both growth and productivity for the total Boeing enterprise."[31]

Meanwhile, McNerney encouraged Boeing's defense unit to tap into the goodwill created by its commercial side. As he pointed out, "While [IDS] is new to India, it has entered the market as a part of Boeing—a known and trusted company. Given the breadth and depth of its capabilities, IDS is uniquely positioned to provide defense products that fit almost all of India's major stated procurement needs. In following an integrated approach to doing business in this market, we are bringing 'the best of Boeing' to India and 'the best of India' to Boeing and our customers . . . and we are replicating this effort in many countries around the world."[32]

HE MAKES ACQUISITIONS THAT COMPLEMENT ORGANIC GROWTH

Despite his emphasis on organic growth, McNerney makes acquisitions that complement the organic growth. At 3M, McNerney purchased Corning Precision Lens (CPL), a manufacturer of lens systems for projection televisions, to build on 3M's strengths in optical systems. The CPL purchase added to 3M's optical product line for the rapidly growing projection TV market. At Boeing, McNerney has sought out acquisitions that complement its aircraft business. For example, he purchased aircraft parts and services provider Aviall as a way to bolster Boeing's already strong position in the provision of aircraft services. He uses acquisitions to strengthen businesses that are already growing organically. Simply put, McNerney will buy a company if it adds sales to an existing business. He won't buy a company to create a new business that does not exist already within the company.

McNerney made the CPL acquisition to add to 3M's optical product line. These products included a long list of films that enhanced the visual quality of various displays. For example, 3M's optical products included brightness enhancement films for electronic displays, traffic control devices, electronic surveillance products, and films that protect against counterfeiting. This was already a significant business for 3M. The growing and profitable division generated 2002 sales of $3.84 billion, up 8.9 percent from

2001. During the same period, that division's operating income increased nearly 32 percent to $915 million.[33]

McNerney saw a big potential market for optical products used in projection TVs. Although 3M's optical product line included some of the projection TV components, it did not sell others that projection TV manufacturers demanded. In order to offer a broader product line to these manufacturers, in December 2002, 3M completed its CPL acquisition. McNerney saw the CPL acquisition as a way to complement 3M's organic growth. As he said at the time, "Really what it does is helps us drive what we were doing anyway, which is drive a terrific graphics business that we had [within 3M's Optical Systems Division]. And as we see technologies coming together, we thought CPL would be a nice addition. So it enhances our organic growth and yet adds—a perfect acquisition for us."[34]

The CPL deal is a good example of McNerney's idea of a complementary acquisition. To satisfy McNerney, a complementary acquisition must pass three tests:

- **The acquisition target should compete in a big, fast-growing market.** McNerney likes to acquire companies in large, rapidly growing markets with significant profit potential.
- **The acquisition should provide capabilities that help the company gain a bigger share of that market.** McNerney wants to acquire companies that bring skills that fit with company strengths. The idea is to create a new competitor that can take a bigger share of the market than either could standing alone.
- **The acquirer should not overpay for the target.** McNerney avoids "shopped deals" because he does not want to get involved in an auction situation that would lead to a higher price. He prefers to negotiate directly with a potential target

to develop a shared rationale for the deal and keep the purchase price in a reasonable range.

Comments by the key executives involved with the CPL deal suggest that it passed these three tests. As McNerney said at the time, "This transaction affirms our strategy of accessing fast-growing markets by acquiring companies with strong market positions and technologies that we can leverage with our own strengths to drive faster long-term organic growth. Combining this business with 3M Optical Systems Division will broaden our technology position in the global display industry."[35]

Exactly how did CPL fit with 3M's strengths? CPL added lenses for rear-projection TVs to 3M's optical film strengths. And 3M believed that the combination of these capabilities would create a formidable competitor in the liquid crystal display (LCD) TV market. As Andy Wong, division vice president of 3M's Optical Systems Division, said, "Adding CPL's technology for rear projection televisions to 3M's full spectrum of display technologies enhances our business, and will accelerate our growth in the current and next generation consumer television applications. Lens systems for large-screen, rear-projection televisions are a great complement to our strong optical film capabilities, which are well-suited to the emerging consumer LCD television segment, a segment expected to grow 56 percent between 2002 and 2006."[36]

Finally, 3M's purchase price for CPL was considered reasonable in light of the size of the market opportunity. 3M paid $850 million in cash for the $260 million (2002 sales) CPL division. 3M had no intention of cutting its 1,500 staff or replacing CPL's executives. With a 600,000-square-foot plant, CPL was the world's largest manufacturer of these specialty lenses. As 3M spokeswoman Donna Fleming said, "We feel strongly that part of the success of the business is due to the strong leadership and the leadership team for the business will remain intact."[37]

Despite his complementary acquisitions, such as CPL, McNerney persisted in emphasizing the centrality of organic growth to 3M. As he said at the time, "I think 3M is all about organic growth. It has been historically. I look out into the future; organic growth is going to be more highly valued than any kind of growth. I think if you look at people that are highly valued by the market today they tend to be organic growers. Now, that doesn't mean we won't do some deals, won't make some acquisitions. But like the Corning deal, it will be done in light of continuing to enhance our organic growth. This is what this company does best and we are spending a lot of time and effort on it. It's a way of controlling what we can control and we feel good about our prospects in this regard."[38]

At Boeing, McNerney has followed a similar approach to complementary acquisitions, using them to boost Boeing's organic growth. As he has said, "Where necessary, we intend to accelerate our organic growth through disciplined acquisitions to expand our capabilities, geographic reach or market access. In fact, in 2006 we made several important niche acquisitions that are helping contribute to support-services growth in both our commercial and defense businesses."[39]

One such acquisition was Boeing's $1.7 billion cash purchase of Aviall in May 2006. Boeing bought the industry's biggest independent provider of new aviation parts and services so it could accelerate its growth in a $25 billion industry where it was already a major competitor. Aviall had 2005 revenue of $1.3 billion and expected 25 percent growth in 2006. Analysts thought the acquisition would help offset the slowdown of typically cyclical commercial aircraft purchases. According to J. B. Groh, an analyst with D.A. Davidson & Co., "when demand for newer aircraft drops off in Boeing's currently growing, but cyclical commercial aviation business, [Boeing] will benefit as parts will be needed for aging aircraft."[40]

The acquisition was intended to expand Boeing's Commercial Aviation Services business, which had been growing at double-digit rates. That business, with 2005 sales of roughly $3.3 billion, delivers materials to airline customers and works with suppliers to maintain spare parts and supply them as needed. In 2005, Boeing also provided roughly $9 billion worth of parts and supply chain management services to its commercial and defense customers. McNerney saw the deal as adding "modestly to earnings in 2007." Furthermore, he said, "It's a very good fit with our existing services business and with our growth strategy. I see tremendous internal and external growth potential for Boeing in this area."[41]

McNerney expects Boeing to continue making niche acquisitions. As he has said, "I think there's a whole host of them within the services thrust. [These include] training, logistics, software and niche technologies. We have a broad ambition, so filling out specific pieces is what you'll see us doing. We have a robust pipeline of opportunities, and it will be a make-versus-buy assessment as we go through. I don't see some big transforming acquisition. You never want to acquire things because of your inability to grow yourself. You want to acquire things to supplement and accelerate the growth plans you've got. Hopefully we'll hold on to that discipline."[42]

McNerney's emphasis on growth through people, rather than deals, offers several benefits:

- **It is more likely to generate consistent profit growth.** If a company can continually come up with new products that can outearn the cost of capital required to design, build, and distribute them, then it's far more likely to exceed investors' profit growth expectations on a consistent basis.

- **It enables a company to control its own destiny.** It pushes executives to set goals and overcome the internal obstacles that might impede those goals. Since effective new-product development inherently demands the cooperation of different functions within a company, when the CEO demands organic growth, the organization must overcome any barriers to such cooperation. As a result, the company learns how to generate growth without depending on other companies. Such growth is more predictable and sustainable.

- **It minimizes the risk that big capital outlays will reduce shareholder value.** When a company invests capital in internal projects, it has a much better understanding of the risks and rewards than if it makes an acquisition. There are two reasons for this: First, when investing in internal projects, the CEO knows the people, the processes, and the technology that will be used. Second, when a company acquires, the risk is far greater that a large amount of capital will be spent all at once and that many unpleasant surprises, such as weak or poorly motivated people, accounting and systems problems, an unpromising R&D portfolio, or difficulty integrating the acquired company, will come to light after that capital has been spent. For these reasons, investing in organic growth is less likely to create a situation in which large amounts of capital yield disappointing returns.

- **It builds the company's portfolio of capabilities.** By keeping pressure on the company to generate growth organically, the CEO forces people to be aware of competitors' capabilities in areas such as engineering, manufacturing, logistics, and sales and to make the investments needed to stay ahead of these competitors. Only by enhancing its capabilities can the company sustain its ability to grow organically.

- **It enhances the management team.** McNerney also uses acquisitions to enhance the management skills of the companies he leads. For example, when he acquired CPL while leading 3M, McNerney wanted to keep the CPL people because he believed that they would add to 3M's portfolio of capabilities. These capabilities were an important asset that McNerney believed would add to 3M's ability to compete in the future. When McNerney makes acquisitions, he views the targets' executives as a source of growth potential.

CONCLUSION

Jim McNerney boosted revenues and profits at 3M and Boeing. At 3M he achieved these results by channeling the company's creative culture to develop new products that could take a meaningful share of rapidly growing markets. And at Boeing, McNerney oversaw enormous investments in new products, which led to substantial order backlogs and significant profit growth. While he used acquisitions in both companies, they complemented existing lines of business and more than paid for themselves through the higher profits they generated.

CHAPTER 7.

TACKLE CHALLENGING SITUATIONS QUICKLY AND EFFECTIVELY

With CEOs' average tenures down to about 4.5 years from about 8.5 years not so long ago,[1] there are always many CEOs who, figuratively or literally, just walked in the door. That's why Jim McNerney's ability to take on new challenges provides such valuable lessons. McNerney's training as a consultant at McKinsey and as a leader at GE prepared him well for parachuting into challenging situations, getting the lay of the land, figuring out the most important things to get done first, and working with people to get the needed results.

McNerney has used these skills well at 3M and Boeing. McNerney was the first outsider ever to run 3M. He quickly cut five thousand jobs and focused research spending on health care products and plastic films for display screens. This was a big contrast with 3M's prior CEOs, who had let its research and development employees work on whatever innovations they wanted without focusing on the revenues they might generate for 3M. McNerney shifted the culture to say, "Give me your three best ideas." And he almost immediately started getting results.

McNerney's focus on a critical few fixes at Boeing helped boost Boeing's revenues and profits significantly, as we saw in table 1 in the introduction. For example, he cut to five from twenty the number of days Boeing takes to close its books each quarter. And, as he did at 3M, McNerney has channeled Boeing's spending into areas where it's likely to get the biggest returns. For instance, Boeing has scaled back research into planes seating fewer than one hundred people, which Boeing doesn't make. Boeing's jetliner unit had already reduced its head count by half and closed Seattle-area factories while continuing to satisfy market demand. Meanwhile, McNerney designated Albaugh to lead an effort to eliminate duplication and get better prices on inputs such as titanium in Boeing's $4.2 billion annual procurement budget.[2]

McNerney's accomplishments at both 3M and Boeing testify to his ability to tackle challenging situations quickly and effectively.

- **He diagnoses problems quickly and effectively.** McNerney has built on his consulting experience and his subsequent management roles to hone his ability to tackle things quickly. He doesn't shy from challenges. He doesn't put things off. He doesn't waste time.
- **He pushes multipronged solutions and avoids simple answers.** McNerney resists the one-size-fits-all approach to management problems. He understands the complex causes of problems and finds solutions to address them.
- **He uses a hard-headed, soft-hearted approach to people.** To accomplish change, McNerney does two things: He first sets very specific goals—the hard-headed part—and then he helps people achieve the goals—applying his soft-hearted side. He also recognizes that not all employees will succeed, and he is honest when letting go employees who aren't working out.

HE DIAGNOSES PROBLEMS QUICKLY
AND EFFECTIVELY

McNerney excels at quickly sizing up a business situation and assessing which problems are most critical. Some executives tend to focus on the problems that they think they can most easily fix, but McNerney is objective in looking for the most urgent problems and tackling them directly.

At GE, McNerney honed his technique for diagnosing problems quickly. As a high-potential manager, McNerney changed jobs every two or three years. This allowed him to build relationships with people across GE's business units, but it also required him to build new relationships quickly. Also, as a rising GE executive, he routinely attended meetings and interacted with the executives in other GE business units. Over the years, these meetings, often convened by CEO Jack Welch, involved McNerney and the other executives in diagnosing and solving a broad array of business problems.[3]

McNerney's networking skills are critical in helping him diagnose business problems, especially when he arrives in a new management job. That's because when he starts a new job, he really doesn't know his direct reports very well. Networking enables him to get an accurate reading about which ones he can trust and which ones he can't.

Sometimes he gets help from people he has met in different environments. For example, when he arrived at GE Aircraft Engines in 1999, through his networking McNerney had already developed a relationship with an executive there whose judgment he trusted.[4] So, when he arrived and began asking his subordinates about how the business was operating, he had someone to help him figure out whose reports were likely to be more, or less, reliable. In cases where he does not have a trusted insider, his unintimidating personal demeanor helps him get to know people and find those in the new unit he can trust. But whatever the situation, one of the first tasks he sets himself is to assess his players and develop what he calls a pyramid of trust. He maps out whose analysis is worth listening to and whose is less reliable, and he tends to replace those at the bottom of that pyramid.[5]

McNerney combines intellect and judgment to learn about the business. According to a retired GE executive, "He was great at asking questions and was a quick learner. He doesn't work on the fringe. He figures out what are the key indicators in the business and he homes in on how those are doing." In the aircraft engine business, McNerney realized that an engine's fuel consumption was a key indicator. There was an opportunity to improve sales by producing engines that consumed less fuel. The retired GE executive continues, "Jim would learn the three to four key factors in each of the business disciplines—finance, engineering, production, and sales—and he would ask questions. And Jim was really good with customers. He met with them and wanted to understand their business."[6]

McNerney tracks indicators that help him to locate the key problems and opportunities within the business. At GE Aircraft Engines, for example, McNerney asked broad-ranging questions. According to the retired GE executive, these included "Are our customers satisfied with our products and service? What improvements do we need to make? What are the trends in our market share? What is our market share forecast? What are the trends in pricing—are we raising or lowering our prices? Is the customer happy with our quality? What new products are our competitors working on? How much are they spending on R&D? Are our product deliveries ahead, on, or behind schedule? Are our new programs ahead, on, or behind schedule? Are we holding our prices on spare parts? How are we doing on meeting our profit targets and getting our costs down? How are we doing on paying and training people?"[7] McNerney used the answers he received to diagnose what was wrong and decide what kind of corrective action to take.

McNerney used a similar approach when he arrived at 3M. He was happy to discover that many of the managers there were amenable to, if not eager for, change. These managers understood that 3M needed to be revived, and McNerney brought with him the leadership needed to diagnose its problems and work with 3Mers to make solutions happen. As McNerney said, "I found a company who thought they weren't achieving all they could, and they were willing to team up with somebody to do more. That was a surprise."[8] However, while McNerney enjoyed support from some of its newer people, he faced opposition from 3M's old guard, who wanted to keep things the way they were.

McNerney impressed 3M's managers as a strong outsider who could restore discipline and focus. When he started work there in January 2001, the economy was in a recession, which actually made painful decisions easier. He quickly realized that 3M would need to both cut costs and boost revenue by focusing its R&D on markets that offered the greatest revenue and profit potential. After rounds of cost cutting, layoffs, and repositioning 3M into fields with greater profit potential, such as health care, 3M achieved record results within several years. By 2003, 3M profits had climbed 35 percent to $2.4 billion on sales of $18.23 billion. 3M's stock price, at $81 a share, was also up 35 percent.[9]

McNerney's keen awareness of the fundamental changes in the economy helped him to diagnose the problems 3M faced. 3M's board brought McNerney in at a time when his predecessor's overly optimistic forecasts about growth were about to be exposed. In September 2000, hosting his last biennial conference for analysts and investors, McNerney's predecessor, L. D. DeSimone, forecast an 11 percent increase in revenue in the year ahead and a 12 percent rise in operating income. DeSimone predicted that 3M's telecommunications business would do even better, with sales and profits surging 25 percent as customers strung more and more fiber-optic lines.[10]

To be fair, DeSimone was not the only executive to think that the telecommunications boom would continue for years. But with the collapse of the dot-com bubble, telecommunications companies would not be able to obtain the debt financing needed to continue to fuel the growth that DeSimone had forecast. And by 2001's first quarter, 3M's operating earnings were tumbling in every business except consumer and office products. The abrupt downturn proved that 3M's business was performing far more weakly than DeSimone had predicted. This created a sense of crisis that gave McNerney a chance to accelerate his change initiatives. As McNerney said, "I showed up in December of 2000, actually, with a business plan that was already irrelevant because the global markets had tanked." All at once, he noted, "we were all in this together." Quickly, and with little dissent, he ordered a cut of five thousand, or 6.6 percent, in 3M's work force.[11]

McNerney was able to tap into a trusted person—as he had at GE Aircraft Engines—when he arrived as Boeing's CEO. That's because while heading GE Aircraft Engines, McNerney had sold jet engines to then–Boeing Commercial Airplanes head Alan Mulally. Mulally was very helpful to McNerney in giving him the inside story on Boeing's executives. This helped McNerney figure out whom he could trust during his first year as Boeing's CEO. By the time Mulally left for Ford's CEO position, McNerney had a good sense of the players at Boeing.[12]

Of course, McNerney cannot always rely on trusted insiders to help him size people up. When that's the case, he uses his disarming personality to put people at ease. McNerney nurtures an environment of respect at his companies. Rather than lording over them his higher rank, McNerney finds common ground with people at all levels of the company. By treating people with respect, he earns theirs. And in so doing, McNerney encourages them to open up about what's going well and what's not. As he meets with people up and down the line, McNerney compares what he hears from low-level people with the answers he receives from his direct reports. If the two agree, he gains confidence in his direct reports.

At Boeing, rather than starting off issuing orders, McNerney spent his first six months talking to employees to get a real understanding of the businesses. He didn't yell or publicly humiliate anyone. Despite the ethical problems we'll explore further in chapter 10, McNerney didn't replace Boeing's top ranks with colleagues from GE. As we saw earlier, McNerney encouraged teamwork and praised then-CEO contender Mulally. He is also good at remembering the names of lower-level people. As a former GE peer said, "Jim's problems have been as tough, or tougher, than the ones that [former GE colleague] Bob [Nardelli] had to face at [Home Depot]. But he has tried to solve them in a much more pleasant way. The guy is loved over there at Boeing—and that's got to make a difference."[13]

McNerney does a great job of diagnosing business problems. His success suggests four lessons for leaders:

- Develop networking skills to help assess people quickly.
- Diagnose critical business problems early.
- Question and learn from your direct reports and find out what business indicators matter most in each function.
- Track changes in those business indicators over time.
- Analyze why they are changing.

HE PUSHES MULTIPRONGED SOLUTIONS
AND AVOIDS SIMPLE ANSWERS

McNerney's long experience as a general manager has taught him to see how the different pieces of an organization interact. If, as in many companies, McNerney had risen to a general management position after spending a career in a specific function, such as sales or engineering, he might have tended to favor a particular functional solution when he became a general manager. Similarly, if he had spent his entire career within a specific line of business—for example, 3M's health care division—then he might have tended to favor that division when it came to allocating resources.

However, thanks to McNerney's decades of experience leading complex organizations, he finds solutions that engage the entire organization rather than favoring one part over another. He can see the benefits of both the analytical and process-driven approach to a business problem and the softer, human side. His contribution comes from the way he can combine both to improve results.

At GE's Aircraft Engines unit, McNerney used the diagnostic process of asking probing questions about such things as pricing and market share trends to pinpoint a significant competitive threat. Specifically, aircraft engine manufacturers had adopted a form of the razor manufacturers' business strategy: Sell the razor at cost and make the profits on the blades. For aircraft engine makers, this translated into selling the engines at a discount—of, say, $5 million to $6 million—and making the majority of their profit (roughly four times the list price of the engine) from selling spare parts and service over a twenty- to twenty-five-year period.[14]

But McNerney discovered that GE was facing a problem with this business strategy. Competitors such as Pratt & Whitney were copying GE's spare parts—engine turbine blades, for example—and selling the spare parts for a fraction of what they cost GE. That's because the parts were not patented and these competitors had not incurred the R&D costs to develop them. McNerney saw that if this trend continued, GE Aircraft's business strategy would need to be overhauled in order to meet its profit goals. McNerney quickly discerned that this threat of losing share in the parts market was a critical challenge for GE.[15]

But this was not the only challenge McNerney faced at GE Aircraft Engines. He identified between fifty and one hundred problem areas, which he categorized as critical, moderate, or minor. He decided that the parts problem was critical because it threatened to cut into GE's revenues, which would make it tough for GE Aircraft to meet the goals in its business plan.[16]

McNerney decided that the solution was to put together a team, including legal, production, and engineering people, and give it the task of developing a new generation of patented spare parts for GE's aircraft engines. These parts would better meet customer needs, and it would be illegal for competitors to copy them. And after about six months, the team developed some workable concepts, so McNerney asked a finance staffer to develop a budget request for the R&D money needed to develop the concept into a prototype.[17]

At Boeing, McNerney employs a similar emphasis on growth and productivity. As at 3M, he has tightened processes and linked executive pay to results. He encourages Boeing's top executives to focus on sharpening its business processes in both defense and commercial airplane manufacturing. He also pays managers based on the financial results he expects them to control.[18]

And McNerney not only works well with his executives, he also improves his relationships with unions. For example, Mark Blondin, president of Machinists District Lodge 751, representing about nineteen thousand Boeing employees in the Seattle area, says of McNerney, "He's got a clean slate with us so far. Whether it's him doing a good job, the economics of the industry, a little bit of luck, hard work or all of the above, the company's doing well since he's been in there."[19]

Wall Street analysts also give McNerney good reviews. As Blondin notes, McNerney benefits from factors that analysts perceive to be outside his control. However, Wall Street analysts credit him with a positive change in management style. Peter Jacobs, an analyst for Ragen MacKenzie in Seattle, has said, "At the one-year point, Jim McNerney's contribution has mainly been in returning credibility to the corporate office. He has raised the ethical bar and put into place things to prevent some of the misdeeds of the past." And Cai von Rumohr of SG Cowen Securities calls McNerney a stabilizing influence at Boeing. Says von Rumohr, "I think his style, which is a little more low-key, giving the heads of his businesses their day in the sun instead of hogging the microphone, has helped bring the company together."[20]

As these comments suggest, McNerney has tackled Boeing's challenges with an unusually strong degree of attentiveness to the human side of management. And he has used his ability to motivate people and to engage Boeing's top leaders in broad corporate initiatives to improve Beoing's financial performance. McNerney instituted "an intense but equal pursuit of productivity and growth" through four management initiatives that he introduced at Boeing's annual executive retreat in Orlando, Florida, in January 2006. He assigned a top executive to head each initiative, intended to cut costs and raise productivity in a specific area:

- **Internal support services productivity.** McNerney saw the potential to make Boeing's corporate services—such as Human Resources and Information Technology—more efficient.

To capture this efficiency, McNerney assigned Boeing's CFO, Jim Bell, to oversee a management initiative to improve Boeing's internal support services.

- **Supply chain efficiency.** McNerney believed that Boeing could tighten the way parts flow into its manufacturing facilities. To that end, he assigned Albaugh to make Boeing's supply chain more efficient.
- **Production improvement.** McNerney saw an opportunity to reduce the time and cost to manufacture Boeing's products. So he put Mulally in charge of improving Boeing's production.
- **R&D ROI.** McNerney wanted Boeing to earn higher rates of return on investment (ROI) in its R&D activities. To achieve this goal, McNerney assigned Boeing's technology chief, Jim Jamieson, specific responsibility for boosting the efficiency and effectiveness of Boeing's R&D programs.[21]

McNerney's use of a multipronged approach to solving problems suggests five lessons for leaders when taking over a new leadership challenge:

- View the organization from the perspective of all its constituents.
- Avoid imposing solutions just because they worked in the past. Tailor an approach to fit the unique problems of the organization.
- Recognize that boosting financial results is crucial to gaining the confidence of constituents.
- Engage constituents in the short-term and longer-term efforts to boost performance.
- Use intellectual humility to tackle challenges, because it builds credibility with constituents and yields better solutions.

HE USES A HARD-HEADED, SOFT-HEARTED APPROACH TO PEOPLE

McNerney recognizes that it's impossible for him to get the results he wants all by himself. So he pays careful attention to engaging others throughout the organization. He sets high expectations for the people who report to him. He gives people direct feedback, and if they're not working as well as he thinks they should, he tells them how he expects them to change. This intellectually tough approach is soft-hearted in the sense that it is honest and gives people a chance to improve.

McNerney believes strongly that leaders should exhibit the values that they want to encourage in others. He starts with himself. When he takes a new job, he works openly and honestly with people in the organization to establish a clear set of shared values. Once the values are established, he expects the leaders below him to model the values in their work. He rewards those who meet his expectations and works with those who don't to help them improve or to find opportunities elsewhere.

At GE Aircraft Engines, he engaged others to solve the spare-parts problem. The people who worked on the team to develop the new patented parts felt confident that there was an implicit contract between themselves and McNerney. If they succeeded in coming up with what McNerney asked of them, a new line of spare engine parts, then he would recognize their contribution when it came time to give out promotions and raises.[22] Perhaps more important, he energized people by encouraging them to come up with the solution to an important problem rather than asking them to simply carry out an order he had issued.

At Boeing, McNerney changed the performance appraisal system to get people on board with the many programs he initiated to solve Boeing's problems. McNerney criticized the tendency he saw at Boeing for managers to be "nice" to people by giving every employee an above-average rating. McNerney echoed his mentor, Jack Welch, who said many times that he thought it was far more humane to let weak performers know early in their careers so they could move on to a different place that might value their skills more highly.

But McNerney had his own way of articulating this concept. As he says, "Accepting such a 'human' result, while not uncommon, is wrong in two obvious ways. First, you get what amounts to grade inflation. If you rate the majority of employees as 'above average,' you undervalue the work of those who ought to be recognized for truly superior performance. And second, you aren't really doing under-achievers or even solid performers any favors by turning D's into C's or C's into B's."[23]

McNerney continues, "Just the opposite: You are depriving them of potentially valuable feedback. In lulling employees into a false sense of security, you are setting them up for the eventual realization, which may not happen well into or even late in their careers that they have been in the wrong place, frustrated and unhappy. And by then, it may be too late for them to do anything to rectify the situation. I've seen it happen to a number of people throughout my career."[24]

McNerney has also seen how people can improve their performance when they receive realistic feedback. As he says, "I've also seen average performers blossom after hearing candid feedback. One employee, who had always had 'you're-doing-great' performance reviews, asked me if he should resign after our first review. I said 'No, it's time to start, not finish! You should work on improving your leadership skills.' And he did! Nobody had ever really helped him understand where he fell short, so he had no way of knowing how he could truly excel, which, by the way, he went on to do."[25]

Finally, McNerney stresses the importance of honest communication. As he argues, "An open culture cannot work without reality-based communication, honest and respectful conversation. That is why the candid, constructive, one-on-one discussion between a manager and his or her direct reports is an essential element in developing people and achieving strong performance within an open culture. Done well, it is that interaction, more than anything else, that engages people's hearts and minds, which excites them and moves them forward."[26]

McNerney's record of tackling challenging situations quickly and effectively suggests three leadership lessons:

- **Take a fresh look at the challenges facing a company.** Along with the pressure to perform, the new CEO gets the benefit of being able to take an independent look at the strategy, organization, systems, and culture nurtured by the previous CEO. For a trained analyst such as McNerney, such an opportunity yields practical insights about what can be done to improve the company's results quickly.

- **Devise effective solutions to the company's problems.** In evaluating these improvement opportunities, an effective CEO realizes that in order for new strategies to bear fruit, they must be "owned" by the organization rather than imposed on it from above. While some CEOs exert power in this way, McNerney believes that a top-down approach is less effective because it fails to exploit the creative talent of the entire organization.

- **Boost results quickly—thus building enthusiasm for ongoing change.** If the CEO devises smart new strategies and tactics and sets high expectations, then the odds are good that results will improve. Shareholders respond by bidding up the company's stock price. And employees see possibilities for career advancement created by the company's improved financial and competitive position. As a result, the pressure for improvement ratchets up as the organization begins to believe it can meet those higher expectations.

CONCLUSION

McNerney quickly tackled the specific challenges he faced in his early months at 3M and Boeing. McNerney diagnosed the companies' most significant opportunities for improvement. He worked with people in the companies to help them see the value of these opportunities and held them accountable for improving results. He communicated his expectations for profit growth to investors, which added to the pressure on his people. When the organization delivered results that exceeded investors' expectations, people were motivated to achieve more.

CHAPTER 8.

TIGHTEN OPERATIONS WITH PROCESS-IMPROVEMENT TOOLS

Looking back over his first two years at 3M, Jim McNerney told a reporter in late 2003, "In the old world—the '70s, '80s and '90s—you could get away with either running the place very productively . . . or growing. In today's world, our overall business objectives are to be simultaneously strong in operating excellence and unusually strong in organic growth." In the slow-growth environment that 3M faced at the time, McNerney concluded, "you've got to do both well."[1]

As assiduously as McNerney pursues growth, he also seeks productivity. Increasing efficiency is a theme that runs through all of his management and operational programs. He sees it as all connected: If you want profitable growth, you need to work on both the cost part and the growth part. We have already looked at the growth part, so now it's time to look at the cost side.

There are many ways to boost operational efficiency, and McNerney is not married to any one of them. He sees no compelling reason to impose the same approach on every organization. Instead, he examines the company's challenges, determines where there are opportunities to boost its efficiency, and judges which techniques will be most appropriate for achieving the goal. The primary technique he has used at Boeing is one called Lean. At 3M, he instituted Six Sigma, which he had seen work well at GE.

Once he decides which technique fits the company best, he starts to educate people so they share a common language for process improvement. He helps select the process-improvement projects, gives teams the resources they need to succeed, eliminates obstacles, and rewards those who get results.

Lean is a quality-management process that Toyota developed and refined. Lean evolved from the Toyota Production System (TPS), which strives to mass-produce goods more efficiently. Lean reduces waste, human effort, manufacturing space, investment in tools, and engineering time to develop a new product. When combined with Six Sigma, Lean helped Toyota rise from a small player to one of the world's largest automobile manufacturers.[2]

Six Sigma is a quality-control process with a slightly different focus. Six Sigma's goal is to boost the consistency of a process and thereby make it more efficient. The term *Six Sigma*, originally coined by Motorola, refers to the Greek symbol used by statisticians to represent the standard deviation from a mean—which measures how tightly a set of data clusters around the average. A manufacturing plant that produces 2,700 errors per million operates at three-sigma predictability. If the process is improved so that the plant produces only about 3.4 errors per million, the plant operates at *six* sigma.[3] McNerney likes Six Sigma not for its statistical precision but because it gets results. GE, one of its early adopters, says it added $16 billion to its profits in the first five years of Six Sigma's implementation.[4]

SIX SIGMA AT 3M

While McNerney pushed Lean at Boeing, he chose Six Sigma for 3M. McNerney found that 3M's culture was quite amenable to Six Sigma because its people were hungry for a way to boost profits by making operations more efficient. It was also a way to ingrain a way of thinking that maintains the pressure to keep improving. According to Laurie Altman, a Six Sigma Black Belt—the designation for those with the highest level of Six Sigma knowledge—at 3M, "Six Sigma is nothing more than a set of statistical tools and processes for problem solving. But it is also about culture change and how an organization thinks about problems, defines them and ensures that the things we are working on are aligned with our business strategy."[5]

McNerney personally led the Six Sigma process at 3M. He participated in training 3Mers in Six Sigma; picked the leaders of 3M's Six Sigma initiatives; helped select the Six Sigma projects on which they would focus; and committed to investors how much 3M's Six Sigma initiatives would boost 3M's bottom line. 3M's shares rose in December 2000 when it announced McNerney's hiring because investors expected him to apply GE's then-respected productivity programs to the more leisurely paced 3M.[6]

McNerney's Six Sigma push achieved tangible results quickly—fulfilling investors' expectations of greater productivity at 3M. By February 2001, one hundred of 3M's top executives had been trained in Six Sigma. And by April 2001, 3M had already started thirty-five Six Sigma projects and one hundred more were scheduled. Moreover, McNerney promised Wall Street that these programs would pay off for 3M—cutting procurement costs by 2 percent in 2001, consolidating suppliers, and moving more of 3M's procurement onto the Web. He had already saved $16 million a year by reducing the types of packages 3M's businesses use.[7]

McNerney played an active role in picking 3M's Six Sigma projects. He focused on three broad areas: accelerating the pace of getting products to market, improving cash flow, and boosting productivity. Teams identified one hundred projects to tackle. And the projects that McNerney and the teams jointly selected got results. McNerney estimates that its Six Sigma projects, together with four other corporate initiatives, cut $300 million from 3M's costs each year. As he said, "I could not be more satisfied [with the results so far]. The people and culture at 3M adapted to Six Sigma faster than any place that I know of."[8]

Thanks to the rapid adoption of Six Sigma after McNerney became CEO, he was able to push projects that covered many different parts of 3M. As he recounts, "We started in our factories and worked on yield, and scrap, and re-work—and got tremendous productivity out of it. Then we moved into our backrooms: finance, and HR, and our customer service organizations—and began to get productivity there. And now we're moving toward our customers. We're linking up with our customers, improving processes that we share and offering our customers help to improve some of their business processes."[9]

McNerney's success at 3M suggests three Six Sigma benefits:

- **Teaches people a way to think about business processes.** Six Sigma introduces to people the concept of a business process and helps them to see how they contribute to that process. By giving people the tools for mapping and measuring processes, Six Sigma gives people the power to not only do what they're told, but to step out of their specific roles and see how their work contributes to a broad chain of activities that affects the company's performance.

- **Encourages people to analyze the effectiveness of these processes.** Six Sigma provides the tools that people need to analyze processes—specifically helping them to measure processes' error rates and to probe into the sources of those errors. These analytical tools generate evidence and insight that people can use to recommend ways to improve processes. In particular, Six Sigma helps people make the case that the improvements they recommend will result in tangible improvements, such as lower costs or increased effectiveness.

- **Gives people the resources they need to improve the processes.** Thanks to a combination of the CEO's support of Six Sigma and the evidence and insight the Six Sigma project teams generate, they are often able to get the money, technology, people, and management support they need to put their recommended improvements into effect.

LEAN AT BOEING

When McNerney arrived at Boeing, many parts of the company were already using Lean techniques. So, building on that, he extended the Lean principle from Boeing's own factories into its partners' factories. Extending Boeing's process and methodologies to suppliers presented a challenge. But McNerney believed that using common measures would improve communications and enhance the overall effectiveness of Boeing's supply chain. Since 1999, Lean principles have helped cut in half the time it takes to assemble a 737—from twenty-two days to eleven days. As a result, Boeing has saved hundreds of millions of dollars and increased its production capacity without adding new facilities.[10]

Boeing's use of Lean thinking has helped reduce its costs and make its processes more efficient and effective. Here are five things McNerney does to achieve these improvements:

- He seeks out waste.
- He educates all participants.
- He gets close to the workers.
- He empowers workers.
- He redesigns processes to focus on value-added activities.

He Seeks Out Waste

Lean's goal is to find and eliminate inefficiency. To infuse Boeing with his ideas about Lean culture, McNerney has encouraged people to use its classification system to find waste in Boeing's production processes. The classifications include seven different kinds of waste, such as **inventory** (parts piling up before finding their way into a product) and **waiting** (a partially assembled product sitting on the factory floor until workers are ready to continue to the next stage).[11] Boeing has found ways to apply the classification system to its own production operations and to that of its suppliers.

At its most basic level, McNerney's Lean culture empowers Boeing's production floor workers to eliminate wasted cost and time from its manufacturing processes. For example, it enabled Beth Anderson, director of the Interiors Responsibility Center (IRC) in Boeing's Everett, Washington, facility that makes overhead stow bins, sidewalls, and ceilings for all commercial airplanes, to choose the less expensive of two identical parts. The ability for a person at Anderson's level to make this simple choice is at the core of Lean's value. According to Anderson, when a mechanic came up to her with the two parts, she thought, "This one costs $2.50 and this one costs $17. So why am I using the one that costs $17?" This simple decision was in part the result of following a Lean ideal that good leaders must understand the daily work in great detail. It was with that thought in mind that she moved her office onto the factory floor.[12] That move enabled her to be closer to the action so she could find waste and take action to remove it from Boeing's processes.

It isn't an easy job to extend the notion of seeking out waste in a simple manufacturing process to a global network of suppliers. The concept is simple: Boeing's suppliers and customers will work with Boeing to seek out and remove waste from their operations. But the details are complex. The application requires suppliers and customers to share Boeing's philosophy and really put it to work in their operations. McNerney appointed Shanahan to become vice president and general manager of the 787 program in part because of his skills with Lean principles.[13] A retired GE executive adds that McNerney picked Shanahan because he is "a hard-ass."[14]

Shanahan is applying the Lean mind-set to Boeing's suppliers as it seeks to meet its 2009 production goals for the 787. In applying Lean principles, Shanahan is using a process called structured reviews, which require Boeing and its suppliers to develop a shared understanding of what each party will do to meet ambitious production schedules. Moreover, in conducting these reviews, Shanahan is encouraging Boeing's suppliers to analyze their production processes and to cut waste from their work. The purpose of these Lean workshops is to educate suppliers in Lean principles while at the same time applying these principles to the specific challenges Boeing and its suppliers face as they seek to meet an ambitious deadline. Shanahan has explained these efforts to work with suppliers as follows: "Concurrent to our flight test focus we are planning and preparing for production rate increases that support both our long-term delivery profile and our goal of delivering 109 airplanes by the end of 2009. This involves a broad set of actions that include structured reviews with our partners, conducting Lean workshops to achieve the requisite productivity, and doing detailed method studies to ensure factory sequence and flows are optimized."[15] Ultimately, Shanahan's work with suppliers revealed the need to scale back the goal of delivering 109 airplanes in 2009.[16]

Shanahan believes that Lean principles will help Boeing to meet its production targets. Boeing is hoping it will help its suppliers of structural components meet their delivery dates and Boeing's assembly requirements. Moreover, Shanahan is trying to apply Lean principles to eliminate a specific kind of waste—the so-called traveled work—out of sequence assembly tasks—that adds so much delay to Boeing's 787 production schedule. And he believes that this formal communication process is increasing Boeing's control over the process. As he puts it, "By driving out specified conditions of assembly for each partner, we are now managing traveled work much more effectively and know exactly what is—what traveled work we expect to be receiving. We expect traveled work and its corresponding disruption to continue to decrease and we are seeing evidence of that already."[17]

Ultimately, Boeing is following the Lean principle of getting close to the work. This closeness to the work is what impelled Beth Anderson to move her office. By gaining greater familiarity with the details of work, Shanahan is in a better position to make informed decisions about how best to meet Boeing's production deadlines. As Shanahan describes it, "What we do is we walk through airplane by airplane how many detailed parts they'll be missing, how many detailed fasteners they'll be missing, what are the risks and the issues so that we have a chance to work them. And a lot of it is getting your hands on the detail and at this point in time, we're spending a lot of time having those conversations about what is missing and making sure that the processes that we've put in place are being followed so that we don't have to pay as close attention to every one of those items."[18]

Shanahan leads detailed reviews with lower-level suppliers in order to "get to the bottom" of the sources of waste. While he recognizes this as critical to meeting Boeing's production targets, he is not happy about getting so involved with these "sub tier suppliers." He would have preferred if Boeing's suppliers had been able to apply the same rigor as Boeing in rooting out waste in their operations. However, he accepts as an important part of his job the need to show Boeing's suppliers how to apply Lean principles. And he hopes the time he spends educating suppliers will be an investment that makes Boeing's suppliers more efficient in the future. According to Shanahan, "Unfortunately, I get into very detailed reviews with sub-tier suppliers, and the reviews aren't where I'm grading their homework and saying, 'Why haven't you done this, why haven't you done that?' It's 'What do you need [to] do, what can I provide, how do we make this plan better?' And the conversations are real open and frank, and sometimes I'm doing something that's holding them back, and other times they just haven't asked for help. That's really where we spend a lot of time these days."[19]

While McNerney is the public face of Boeing as it seeks to extend Lean principles to its suppliers, he has delegated the day-to-day management of this to Shanahan. In so doing, he is recognizing a key principle of Lean, which is to empower leaders and workers to drive out waste from operations. Whether McNerney empowered the right people to do this for the 787 will become clearer in 2009, when he has committed to delivering aircraft to customers.

He Educates All Participants

By the time McNerney became CEO, Boeing had a long-established history of using Lean techniques in its manufacturing operations. This history provided a strong foundation on which to build a broader understanding of Lean, both in the parts of Boeing beyond manufacturing and outside Boeing among its suppliers and customers. Because of his history of introducing new management initiatives, McNerney is acutely conscious of the need to educate people in these new techniques. So as a first step in his effort to extend Lean, McNerney started teaching Boeing's Lean "language." Referring to suppliers, McNerney says, "That could be a challenge. They may not have the same process and methodologies as us, but that's one of the ways we're trying to create a family here. We then have common metrics which leads to better communications, and using the same vocabulary just makes the whole thing work better."[20]

With a common language, Boeing and its suppliers could teach and learn from each other. To that end, McNerney established Lean+, a Boeing growth and productivity initiative. One of the most effective parts of Lean+ were the regular meetings McNerney hosted to exchange information. McNerney holds semiannual Lean+ conferences at different Boeing sites, which gather roughly 850 employees who are actively involved in Lean+. His message to Boeing employees and teams is that they need to support the Lean+ initiative and use standardized tools to conduct their work.[21]

Such conferences are the most concentrated way for McNerney to transfer Lean learning. For example, Boeing's May 2007 Lean+ Conference in Costa Mesa, California, asked attendees to learn and share knowledge and best practices across Boeing and with supplier partners and customers. The goal was to improve and solve problems together. Bill Schnettgoecke, vice president and Lean+ leader, told the audience, which included Boeing employees, customers, and industry partners, that Boeing needed to do more to help customers resolve their business challenges. As Schnettgoecke said, "Making Boeing the industry benchmark for productivity will require each of us to align with Lean+ as our one approach; to seek more commonality in our tools, processes and language; and then eliminate the non-standards. Our customers deserve it and they are counting on it."[22]

McNerney underscored the importance of educating Boeing's partners and customers in Lean principles by the importance of the people he invited to the conference. Attendees included McNerney, Boeing Lean leaders, suppliers including the chairman, president, and CEO of Rockwell Collins, and customers such as Ron Ritter, special assistant for Air Force Smart Operations to the secretary of the U.S. Air Force, and deputy director of the Air Force Smart Operations Office. The conference also featured a panel discussion among Employee Involvement team leaders—who run Lean projects—from five Boeing sites. Additionally, during breakout sessions, nineteen employees from different Boeing sites shared how Lean helped boost their productivity.[23]

To initiate organizational change, McNerney educates people. He started by establishing a common language. Then he used that language to transfer Boeing's expertise from manufacturing to other parts of Boeing and to its suppliers and customers. His semiannual meetings of key Lean+ leaders and other participants encourage sharing of best practices and benchmarking.

He Gets Close to the Workers

Once people have learned about Lean, McNerney wants them to put its principles into practice. In order for that to occur, the barriers between workers and their supervisors must tumble. This increases the flow of information and allows the workers on the front lines to be analysts and improvers of the process rather than just cogs in the machinery. Moreover, the free flow of information allows problems and solutions to emerge more quickly, which improves process efficiency and effectiveness.

Through Lean training, McNerney has pushed supervisors to work more closely with workers. He has also personally involved himself in the selection of Lean leaders who will actively foster communication. In McNerney's view, Boeing benefits from collaboration among workers and supervisors in two ways. First, it creates a deeper leadership bench. That's because supervisors who can make their operations work more effectively are good candidates to take on additional management responsibility. Second, by collaborating with workers, such supervisors learn about problems before they become too costly and can generate more effective solutions to those problems once they surface.

Beth Anderson's decision to move her office to the factory floor is one example of a leader seeking to lower barriers. Anderson had spent twenty years as an engineer before taking on a supervisory role. When her boss asked her to prepare a report on how to increase her area's production rate, she realized that she really didn't know much about the details of the operataion. Anderson's initial ignorance about the machines on the production floor—she did not know what a router was—caused gasps among the workers.[24]

But Anderson's openness and willingness to learn made a positive impression on her colleagues. For example, Leanne Jackson, team leader for ceilings and sidewalls, said of Anderson's new office location: "I love that. It makes her more accessible to employees. I think they just feel she's not separate from us, doing her own thing. She's more involved with us in our daily work." Mike Herscher, leader of the Commercial Airplanes Lean Enterprise office, seconds the notion that involvement in daily work is a valuable benefit of Lean. In Herscher's view, "The farther away managers are from the work area, the more it dilutes the information they get."[25]

Lean also encourages information exchange between managers and workers in the form of teaching and learning. McNerney is very much a leader-teacher himself, and he viewed Lean as another way to further infuse teaching and learning throughout Boeing. Herscher witnessed this information exchange firsthand when he accompanied Carolyn Corvi, vice president and general manager of Airplane Production, on her regular weekly walks through production and office areas. Corvi was responsible for managing BCA's production process—including design, production, and delivery.[26]

Once a week, she spent three hours in a work area, accompanied by several students of Lean—hourly, salaried, managers, and executives. They learned from real-life examples and talked to employees about improvements. According to Herscher, "The people will talk about what they're working on, and Carolyn will share the philosophy and principles of [Lean] and challenge them to think how they would adopt principles in their work environment. She teaches, and at the same time, she learns."[27]

As part of Lean, McNerney encourages Boeing supervisors to get closer to workers. This produces important benefits for Boeing. It creates a shared language for process improvement between supervisors and workers. It encourages a freer flow of information about opportunities to improve operations. It spurs collaboration between supervisors and workers to capture those improvement opportunities. And it creates a culture that sustains such improvement.

He Empowers Workers

McNerney also recognizes that the logical extension of getting closer to the work is letting the workers themselves make decisions that improve operations. Once workers have the analytical tools and data they need to analyze their work processes, it makes sense for them to make decisions themselves without waiting for their supervisors. Once they have lowered the barriers between themselves and their supervisors, the flow of communication should be robust, and thus process changes should not come as a surprise to supervisors.

At Boeing, the success of Lean also depends heavily on transferring ownership of its principles to people on the factory floor. For example, Glen Kanenwisher, general supervisor for part of the final assembly of Boeing's 737 in Renton, Washington, shares with Anderson and Corvi the belief that it's important to get to know Boeing's workers. As he says, "You've got to get out of the office, and you've got to know your work force, and they have to know you."[28]

But Kanenwisher highlights an important trait for a manager trying to instill Lean principles in an organization—inspiring employees and "fostering ownership" of their work. *Gemba* is Japanese for "the real place," and a *gemba walk* into work areas is a key part of Lean thinking. Kanenwisher tries to walk through his area and meet with the employees at least twice a day. "I walk up to them, and I learn the issues of the day by asking them how everything is going and if there is anything I can do for them," he said. "You have to be prepared to follow up."[29]

And when he does follow up, he tries to model the right kind of problem-solving behavior, stressing Lean thinking and cooperation. Employees might request help with a supplier issue or a "defect" report on an assembly traveling into their area. Kanenwisher says he is seeing a change in the nature of these requests as employees take ownership. Now, he's less likely to hear about what's wrong—and more likely to hear an employee asking for help making an improvement. Kanenwisher is upbeat about Lean and about continuous improvement. As he said, "I know we are doing well because employees are dissatisfied with the current situation—meaning they want to get dramatically better than they are today. And we're already world class today."[30]

McNerney has created an atmosphere at Boeing that encourages workers to take ownership of what they do. This shift is evident as they change from *identifying problems* to asking their supervisors to help them *implement proposed solutions*. In making this shift, McNerney is tapping into the know-how of Boeing's workers and encouraging them to use that knowledge to improve operations. Rather than waiting for supervisors to solve problems, McNerney creates a culture of leadership where workers solve more of their problems. And that culture radically reduces the time between when a problem is found and when its solution benefits Boeing.

He Redesigns Processes to Focus on Value-Added Activities

The ultimate purpose of McNerney's efforts to educate and empower workers is to change the way Boeing works. Specifically, McNerney seeks to eliminate waste from Boeing's work and use the resources thus freed up to invest in activities that create value for customers. For example, if Boeing can change a process by delaying delivery of components to reduce the amount of time that inventory sits waiting in an assembly plant, then he can make more efficient use of both Boeing's capital and that of his suppliers.

By extending Lean throughout the 787 development process, both Boeing and its suppliers lower their costs and speed up their processes. As McNerney, says, "What we're doing is extending the Lean principle from our own factories into our partners' factories, and there are some tremendous benefits. As people partner with us, we're expecting people to continue on a Lean journey and to share the production with us on behalf of our customers. It's basically an extension outside of our own boundaries."[31]

Boeing works with its suppliers to identify the sources of waste in their joint work. And it pushes a discussion of how best to redesign their processes to cut that waste. As Shanahan describes the process, "When we sit down and do a review with our partners, the review starts with a discussion about their readiness to increase their production rates. So we look at everything from the tooling, do they have sufficient amount of tooling to meet the production rate increases, capital equipment, and power parts. So there are about nine criteria that we review against every one of their production rate increases, and concurrent to this we have our on-site staff doing the background auditing of that information, so it's not like somebody comes online and says, 'Hey, everything's great.' "[32]

Ultimately, Shanahan's goal is to create a clear picture of the improvement opportunities in the operation. He inherited a process where these kinds of conversations did not happen because Bair assumed that the suppliers were doing what Boeing expected unless they told him otherwise. The delays that cost Bair his job revealed that Shanahan could only improve on the situation if he probed aggressively for problems. As he says, "So what we do [is seek] a lot of transparency. The areas that aren't on track, that's where we spend our time reviewing the plan to improve that."[33]

This Lean analysis tightens Boeing's operations. As Shanahan says, "In flushing out the risks, we put improvement plans in place. And that creates this flywheel effect, where everybody gets aligned on the program-level risks that we collectively need to work [on] together to improve their schedule. And it really establishes a battle rhythm and a set of behaviors that allow us to be more integrated and solve these problems."[34]

Learning from Lean

The delay in the 787 production schedule suggests that Boeing is struggling to extend Lean to its suppliers' factory floors. One of the problems is that it has such a long history of applying Lean principles to its own operations that it made the mistake of assuming that when Boeing's suppliers talked about applying Lean, they had that same level of experience. According to a retired GE executive, "From the 1960s to the 1990s, whenever Boeing had a production problem, they would throw people at it. Boeing is a company that will spend money to solve a problem. They will fix it now. It is not a cost-driven company, it is revenue driven."[35]

With this long history, Boeing executives who went to visit suppliers in Italy, China, Japan, and Spain listened to their executives talk about their Lean processes and how they would design, manufacture, and deliver components. And according to the retired GE executive, "Boeing believed these suppliers and assumed that if there was a crunch time, the suppliers would throw five hundred or six hundred people at the problem just as Boeing would."[36]

Unfortunately, Boeing discovered that when crunch time came, the suppliers had a different attitude toward fixing problems than Boeing did. According to the retired GE executive, "The supplier says 'I signed up to hire a hundred people. I'll fix it when I fix it.' The result is that parts start to slip. The suppliers don't have the same focus as Boeing, and people are late. The suppliers preach Lean, but they don't act when it costs them money. Boeing believed that suppliers would act just like they did. Boeing will fix this, but it will be really hard."[37] As we'll explore in chapter 9, that fix has to do with a change in the way McNerney manages—instead of *delegating and trusting*, McNerney *trusts but verifies*.

For McNerney at Boeing, Lean offers the following benefits:

- **Creates a common language between supplier and customer.** Lean provides a well-tested common language for communicating about process effectiveness. It includes tools for analyzing processes, finding what's wasteful in those processes, and eliminating that waste. This common language is a critical starting point for eliminating joint costs and wasted time in the relationship between a supplier and a customer.
- **Provides an effective framework for analyzing processes.** Lean gives manufacturing workers the tools they need to map out processes and to distinguish between parts that add value and parts that don't. In making this distinction, it helps managers think about how to take out excess cost and time from its processes.
- **Provides tested tools for eliminating process waste.** Lean contains the tools needed to match process-improvement approaches to specific sources of waste such as inventory and waiting. The result is that Lean can help cut wasted cost and time out of supplier/customer relationships.

McNerney's efforts to overcome the challenges of extending Lean to its suppliers and customers offer key lessons for leaders, including the following:

- **Trust but verify.** Boeing has learned that it is a mistake to assume that a supplier, in the middle of seeking to conclude a large contract, will objectively describe its strengths *and* weaknesses when it comes to implementing Lean principles. As we'll explore further in chapter 9, Boeing's experience suggests that when attempting to extend Lean to suppliers, it is essential to verify suppliers' claims and to scrutinize not only the supplier but the suppliers' suppliers as well.

- **Balance management initiatives with short-term demands.** McNerney recognized that extending Lean to suppliers would need to be done in a way that did not take time away from the more critical short-term imperative of meeting Boeing's 787 production goals. It appears that Shanahan was quite focused on using those specific aspects of Lean principles that could be applied quickly to help Boeing achieve these production goals more effectively.

CONCLUSION

Jim McNerney improves operating performance by boosting growth and tightening operations. He is familiar with a variety of management tools for boosting productivity and fits the technique to the situation. At 3M, McNerney trained thousands of people in Six Sigma techniques and gave the green light to hundreds of projects that brought hundreds of millions of dollars to 3M's bottom line. And Boeing has enjoyed significant benefits from McNerney's efforts to extend Lean from Boeing's factory to its partners'. The result of McNerney's initiatives to tighten operations has been higher operating margins and more empowered workers at 3M and Boeing.

CHAPTER 9.

PARTNER WITH GLOBAL SUPPLIERS TO REDUCE RISK AND ACCELERATE TIME TO MARKET

The plans for Boeing's 787 were well under way when Jim McNerney became CEO in 2005. It was to be a revolutionary project. To reduce the capital costs and shorten time to market, McNerney's predecessor had already decided to outsource much of the work on the 787. Boeing would be responsible for the overall design and assembly of the aircraft, but a closely aligned network of global suppliers would design and manufacture the components.

Even though the decision on outsourcing was made before McNerney moved into the executive suite, as a Boeing board member, he was an early supporter of the idea. And as CEO he has been responsible for implementing it and overseeing its management. The execution has proved difficult, and the initial 787 delivery date has been repeatedly postponed. But McNerney has persevered, pushed the program to new levels, and learned from his mistakes. As a result, Boeing still expects to start delivering the plane by the end of end of 2009.[1]

The bold notion of transforming global suppliers into global partners required a radical loosening of Boeing's control over the suppliers. Instead of specifying in great detail exactly what each supplier would manufacture, Boeing would only describe what the component should do and let the supplier decide how to design and build it. Boeing has outsourced 70 percent of the design and manufacturing work, much of it to firms abroad. This has meant that for Boeing to meet its production targets, all of those highly complex parts need to come together correctly and on time in Boeing's Everett, Washington, plant. This has presented significant management challenges, one of which was getting dozens of partners around the world working productively on the same design software, linked to the same database with one set of drawings.[2]

Boeing's first attempts at the hands-off approach turned out to be a bit too hands-off. When suppliers had problems, Boeing was too slow to see them and get them resolved. But when the anticipated delivery date had to be postponed several times because of supplier problems, McNerney replaced the person in charge, Bair, and became more involved himself.

Despite the problems, he remains convinced that global partnering is a key to substantial profits, and to capture those profits McNerney has taken the following steps:

- He works closely with suppliers and their subcontractors during design and manufacturing.
- He builds trust up and down the line and with partners.
- He monitors performance relative to schedule and adjusts accordingly.

HE WORKS CLOSELY WITH SUPPLIERS AND THEIR SUBCONTRACTORS DURING DESIGN AND MANUFACTURING

By placing a greater burden for design and manufacturing on its suppliers, Boeing hoped they would share its dedication to meeting deadlines. But at first, Boeing may have handed off too much responsibility to suppliers. They may have had the dedication to meet the deadlines, but some of them began to struggle with the challenges of actually doing it. As these struggles jeopardized delivery schedules, McNerney stepped in to tie Boeing and the suppliers more closely together. One way that he did this was to send teams of Boeing engineers to work with the suppliers at their home locations.[3]

In taking the $10 billion gamble on the 787, Boeing had ambitious goals, and it anticipated some of the risks. But even with contingency plans, Boeing was overly optimistic about its production schedule—to deliver 109 787s by the end of 2009. Boeing believed that this schedule was feasible because it was relying on more than fifty suppliers working twenty-four hours a day at 135 sites on four continents designing and building 787 parts.[4]

This ramp-up in dependence on suppliers represented a significant change in Boeing's approach to making airplanes. Instead of staying true to its legacy as a "wrench-turning manufacturer," Boeing hoped to remake itself as a "master planner, marketer and snap-together assembler of high-tech jetliners." To accomplish all the other activities, Boeing's global suppliers took on responsibilities from detailed design to heavy manufacturing. Boeing anticipated that these partners, working in plants in Japan, China, Italy, and France, would assemble huge airline sections, fill them with electronics, seats, and other components, then airlift them to Seattle. There, Boeing hoped it would be able to snap together all the pieces—built to tolerances of thousands of an inch—in three days. Boeing's objective for this new approach to making aircraft was to cut costs, improve design, and regain its position as the world's biggest aircraft maker.[5]

Boeing's contractual relationships with these partners differed significantly from its traditional ones. Boeing held these partners to strict, fixed-price contracts intended to slash costs and boost productivity. It wanted to tap into their expertise while passing off to the partners roughly half the project's $10 billion of risk.

Initially, some Boeing engineers feared that globalizing product development would lead to a U.S. brain drain, which might create powerful new competitors.[6]

To offset some of the negatives for suppliers, Boeing changed the way it described the work it wanted suppliers to do. In the past, Boeing's work orders had included thousands of pages and required suppliers to "build to print." In other words, build exactly as specified with no variations or exceptions. By contrast, on the 787, work orders were dozens of pages long and describe only what the given part or system should do, not how to build it.[7]

Different partners were responsible for different parts of the 787. For example:

- **Nose.** Boeing's Wichita plant made the 787's nose.
- **Tail.** A joint venture of Italy's Alenia Aeronautica and Vought Aircraft Industries in Dallas was responsible for the tail section.
- **Wing and center section.** Three Japanese companies—Mitsubishi Heavy Industries, Kawasaki Heavy Industries, and Fuji Heavy Industries—built the 787's wing and center sections.

These partners will pack their stuffed sections into two modified 747 airplanes—known as DreamLifters—and airlift them to Everett, Washington. There a small crew of Boeing mechanics will bolt the sections together in the planned three days. This is very fast. Boeing's previous fastest final-assembly process, for the 737 line, was eleven days.[8]

Boeing's experience with the Hamilton Sundstrand unit of United Technologies Corp. illustrates the kinds of benefits that Boeing anticipates from all its suppliers. Hamilton Sundstrand has the assignment to design a power plant and cooling air compression systems for the 787. Although Hamilton found Boeing initially unwilling to relinquish control of key decisions, the two companies eventually worked things out,[9] and the supplier was able to reduce the size of the cooling and refrigeration system by 20 percent. This means less weight, fewer parts, and lower costs. In the electrical system, Hamilton substituted a smaller, solid-state circuit-breaker box for a bulky mechanical one. That freed up space under the passenger deck, creating room for revenue-producing cargo. The changes, which benefited Hamilton (because it was able to boost its margins by lowering its production costs) and Boeing would not have happened if Hamilton merely were building "to print," as in the old days.[10]

Boeing's close working relationship with Hamilton Sundstrand exemplifies what McNerney wants to see with all its 787 suppliers. By sharing information and expertise, the two companies developed better power, air-conditioning, and refrigeration systems than either would have been able to achieve without such collaboration. Hamilton Sundstrand has more knowledge of power and air-conditioning technology than Boeing. However, Boeing has a better understanding of how the power and air conditioning systems need to fit within the 787. By working jointly with Hamilton Sundstrand, Boeing gets a better power, air-conditioning, and refrigeration system on its 787 while bearing less of the financial risk for developing it.

Perhaps one reason that the relationship with Hamilton Sundstrand worked so effectively was that they had worked together in the past. In working with global suppliers on the 787, Boeing created a very diverse and dispersed organization. Boeing wasn't issuing orders, so it needed to develop the softer skills required to influence suppliers working in a different culture and different time zone.[11]

HE BUILDS TRUST UP AND DOWN THE LINE
AND WITH PARTNERS

If all Boeing's suppliers had delivered as well as Hamilton Sund-strand, McNerney would have been quite satisfied with Boeing's approach to working with suppliers. Ultimately, Boeing's outsourc-ing strategy represents a huge leap of faith in others' ability to make realistic promises about what they will do and then doing what's needed to deliver on the promises. For McNerney, as for any leader, it comes down to the simple fact that one person can-not do all the work. The leader must rely on others. And in the case of McNerney's outsourcing strategy, those others include Boeing's program managers, its workers, its suppliers, and its sup-pliers' subcontractors. If each of these groups of people makes promises about what they will do and then fulfill those promises, McNerney's outsourcing strategy achieves its ambitious goals. If there are any gaps between what people promise and what they deliver, then the strategy falls short of the goals.

Observers of Boeing's problems with the 787 fall into two camps. There are those, such as the retired GE executive and Mor-gan Stanley's Wood, who view the situation as a minor and tem-porary glitch. And there are others, such as veteran aircraft industry analysts Wolfgang Demisch and George Hamlin, who see the 787 production delay as the external manifestation of a deeper problem. Ultimately, McNerney recognized that the most fundamental problem was Boeing's culture. When NcNerney be-came CEO, Boeing was a place that was ruled by fear. Nobody wanted to bring bad news up the line because it would damage the messenger's career. McNerney overcame this cultural problem through a new management approach—*trust but verify.*

The most sanguine of the observers is Wood. In her view, the delay in delivering the 787 is a minor glitch. As she says, "The 787 took a $10 billion investment. Building an aircraft is a very serious business. There is one crash in six million flights. If it takes four or five extra months to get it perfect, it's more important to make the aircraft safe than to deliver it fast. These are normal glitches. The 787 is a revolutionary product like Sony's Walkman or Apple's iPod. It's more important for Boeing not to screw up the manufacturing than to get it delivered on time. Boeing is bringing back the magic of flight."[12]

However, Wood suggests that perhaps McNerney should have trusted his instincts about the situation more than the people who reported to him. She notes that, "The 787 delays don't appropriately rest on McNerney. They're not his problem. Boeing was changing the way they built airplanes so significantly. He looked at it with a skeptical eye and decided Boeing shouldn't do this on a compressed schedule. McNerney backed people even though he had his own misgivings. The BCA people told McNerney: 'You're silly to have misgivings. Jim, don't be worried. Trust us.' But as an outsider looking in, I could feel that McNerney was prickly about this situation. He was worried. But he didn't know how to do it because he wasn't an engineer. He needed to empower people and let them figure out how to make it work."[13]

But in October 2006, McNerney decided to make available an additional $500 million in R&D funds to BCA. He anticipated that BCA would need the funds to fix production problems with the 787. However, he also anticipated that BCA would perceive the offer of the capital as an admission that they could not meet the production schedule. As he expected, BCA had mixed feelings about accepting the funds. According to Wood, "BCA was livid. They thought McNerney didn't know anything about airplanes. But soon thereafter, BCA churned through the $500 million. McNerney had misgivings. He needs to trust his gut. But you can't expect a guy in his first twelve to eighteen months on the job [to overrule the experts]. This is really hard stuff, and Boeing is fanatical about detail. They'll delay to get it perfect. If an airplane fails, three hundred people die. This is serious and hard. So another four- to five-month delay is not too bad."[14]

The retired GE executive thinks that Boeing has learned an important lesson from its troubles globalizing the 787's product development. As he says, "Boeing will fix it after having learned a tough, embarrassing lesson: Don't trust your suppliers. Boeing checked out suppliers' plants and Lean processes. But those checking out the suppliers had worked at Boeing for twenty years. They know how Boeing does it. So they put their cultural filter on it. They assume the supplier's plant manager will respond to a problem the same way Boeing would. Boeing would think: 'If I run into a problem, I'm getting a hundred people until I fix the autoclave or the milling process.' Boeing would fix a problem in two weeks, but the suppliers might take longer."[15]

The retired GE executive, like Wood, appears to be cutting McNerney slack in terms of holding him responsible for the 787 delay. He believes that executives lower in Boeing's chain of command should be held responsible. According to the retired GE executive, "Jim is asked a lot of questions, and he will be embarrassed. He's up at the top. You have to look at the people who were directly reporting to Jim. Scott Carson, BCA head, and Mike Bair were telling McNerney, 'Don't worry. We've got this under control.' It's an issue of the management chain of command. Jim will sit down and think 'I'm embarrassed, but I haven't screwed the stockholders. Boeing stock traded at $57 when I took over, it went as high as $107, and now it's at $84—still $30 above where it was when I started.' "[16]

However, the retired GE executive believes that McNerney will demand change and that ultimately nobody will care about a yearlong delay in delivering the 787. As he says, "McNerney's [view is] never again. He'll say, 'Tell me how it's never going to happen again.' People have screwed up. Bair has been relieved of his job. But a year from now, who cares? Boeing didn't deliver in the first quarter of 2008. It will be the third quarter of 2009. In 2010 and 2011 nobody will care."[17]

Other industry analysts view the way Boeing has handled the delay as symptomatic of a company not being honest with itself. According to Hamlin, "Boeing decided to do two things with the 787 which put it on the leading edge. It was not so much the outsourcing that was new—it was new to outsource the production of a non-aluminum-hulled aircraft. Boeing had globalized its component suppliers successfully with the aluminum-hulled 777 and 767. However, with the 787, Boeing did the outsourcing with a new technology—*composites*."[18]

One of McNerney's great accomplishments was convincing these world-class suppliers to accept so much more financial risk than they had in the past. In Hamlin's view, the reason for his success there was simple: "There are only so many really world-class producers. And since there are not very many new product development contracts that come along in the industry, these suppliers were willing to take on the financial risk of designing, building, and delivering these components."[19]

Ultimately, Hamlin thinks that Boeing has taken on too much risk. As he says, "It was the combination of a great array of global suppliers and the leap in technology that made this a new situation for Boeing, which contributed to the production schedule problems. And what it should have done was to call a halt and tell investors and customers that it did not know when the aircraft would be delivered and it would get back to them when it knew. Boeing is not being honest with itself. And it creates bad feelings with the airlines."[20]

Hamlin believes that Boeing needs to be systematic in the way it analyzes the problem and develop a solution. As he says, "Boeing needs to look at the situation like an accident investigation. There

is a need for it to be done urgently, but there is no point in specu-
lating. It needs to wait and answer questions such as: What will it
take to get the program right? When can we get them delivered?
How do we do it right? Some suppliers are on schedule, but others
are not. The problem for the long term is whether Boeing is squeezing suppliers too hard and leaving a bad taste in their mouths.
When it developed the 777, there were many global suppliers, but
it was not as big a technological leap, so there were no production
problems. However, the 787 involves more significant change—
composite materials and snapping the components together in
days. It's hard to achieve such lofty goals."[21]

A European industry insider, however, attributes Boeing's
problems with the 787 production schedule to arrogance. As he
says, "Boeing employed a new strategy for the 787, and it overestimated [what its suppliers could do]. Boeing expected them to work
like Boeing, and that's not realistic. It's a bit of arrogance. If we can
do it in the U.S., our global suppliers can do it as well. Giving suppliers design authority versus telling them exactly what to do was
a big change. There was less risk for Boeing and more investment
on the shoulders of the suppliers. But the suppliers saw an opportunity to recover their investment due to the big market for the
787. However, in trying to deliver, the suppliers in some cases
picked the wrong subcontractors. And for the first six months'
worth of delays, Boeing didn't know what was going on. Delays
went on for a year or more without Boeing really knowing what
was going on."[22]

But Demisch blames a very fundamental lack of trust within
Boeing between leaders and people in operations for the 787 production problems. He sees this lack of trust as affecting the flow of
communication needed to understand the problem and solve it.
Demisch contrasts the 787 problems with the great success Boeing
experienced in the 1960s as it developed the 747. And he concludes
that while both projects were highly innovative for their times,

the way Boeing managed the 747 program presented a compelling example for trust, communication, and understanding up and down the line. In his view, with the 787 that trust broke down.

According to Demisch, "The 747 was the gold standard. It was a huge new plane with new engineering and a new factory. It was one of the riskiest endeavors in Boeing's history, but because of understanding up and down the line, guys knew what the problems were and they communicated through a chain of trust. The 747 experienced major glitches—for example, the engine didn't work. But everybody understood the problem. There was no BS. They knew what they could and couldn't do. It took four years from design to production."[23] The 787, whose design kicked off in 2003, is likely to take at least six years.

Demisch believes that this atmosphere of trust has vanished. Moreover, in his view, senior management talks in the language of numbers and financials while people in engineering and scheduling roles speak a different language. Demisch asks, "What should Boeing do? It's lost that trust up and down the line. The Web site of the Boeing engineering union, the Society of Professional Engineering Employees in Aerospace (SPEEA), discusses a controversy about corporate leadership making noises about getting rid of SPEEA. I can't imagine anything more provocative to highly skilled engineers than Boeing saying, 'You are union and we don't want you.' As it stands, there's a loss of communication and confidence up and down the line."[24]

McNerney recognized that if he wanted to restore the lost trust he would need to change the way he managed each level of the complex organization he had created to implement his outsourcing strategy. The approach he brought to Boeing was to delegate responsibility to a trusted leader and assume that the leader would know which problems could be solved without involving McNerney and which required his attention. McNerney initially applied this delegation logic to Boeing's program manager for the

787. McNerney assumed that Boeing's workers would let the program manager know if they encountered problems with Boeing's suppliers. And he expected Boeing's suppliers to let Boeing know if they experienced problems with their subcontractors.

But the delegation logic that McNerney brought to Boeing did not withstand the reality of the problems Boeing faced with the 787. Bair either did not receive reports of problems from workers or did not convey the reports to McNerney. And many of Boeing's suppliers did not share with Boeing the problems they were encountering in satisfying the terms of their contracts. While McNerney expected to be informed of these problems, the people to whom he delegated let him down.

McNerney responded to the ensuing loss of trust with a new approach—Ronald Reagan's "trust but verify." Under *trust but verify*, McNerney maintains the delegation he used in the past. But he also personally meets with operational people. In those meetings, McNerney looks in their eyes as he asks them how things are going. If they flinch or look away when answering, he knows that there is a problem. And he digs for the truth. If there is a big gap between what his program manager tells him and what he learns from people on the line, he knows that the wrong person is in the program manager job. When McNerney talks to Boeing workers to find out what is going on in operations, he also asks what he can do to help them. Are there any obstacles that he can remove?[25]

In order for this *trust but verify* approach to work, McNerney expects Boeing's program managers to do the same thing with its suppliers. Specifically, Boeing assembled a management team that was assigned to work on site with suppliers as well as in the final assembly facility of the 787. According to Carson, "These additional operational experts will improve our ability to plan, execute, measure and react in a timely way to changing circumstances."[26]

Ultimately, McNerney wants to restore the flow of accurate, timely, and relevant information up and down the line and out to suppliers. This is the way he builds and sustains the trust needed to meet Boeing's 787 production schedule.

How did McNerney develop this concept of delegation? At GE, McNerney used delegation effectively. He described to his people what he wanted to achieve and expected them to carry it out. For the most part, at GE, McNerney's people did not disappoint him. If people encountered difficulties in carrying out McNerney's wishes, they informed him of the challenges they were encountering and proposed a solution. As a result of working effectively in this kind of environment, McNerney grew accustomed to the idea that delegation worked.[27]

Boeing has over 240 programs under way at a time, and it is simply not possible for McNerney to run each of them.[28] He needs to delegate and trust that unless the program managers tell him otherwise, things are going smoothly. However, not all of Boeing's suppliers were able to deliver what Boeing expected them to produce when Boeing expected them to deliver it. The result was that in October 2007 McNerney replaced Bair with Shanahan.

During the first week of October, Boeing announced a six-month delay in deliveries. And McNerney was clearly displeased about this most recent delay, Boeing's third for the 787. "We are disappointed about the schedule changes," McNerney said several times. He went on several times during a teleconference to convey how upset he was about failing to meet customer commitments. Bair paid the price for disappointing him.[29]

The 787 experience has changed McNerney's ideas about how to create and sustain trust in the kind of complex, dispersed organization needed to build an aircraft. McNerney's experience suggests three lessons for leaders:

- Global product development will work if there is trust up and down the line and between the company and its suppliers.
- Such trust evolves from a policy of trusting and verifying.
- If there is a gap between what workers say and what their executives promise, intervene aggressively to resolve the problems.

HE MONITORS PERFORMANCE RELATIVE TO SCHEDULE AND ADJUSTS ACCORDINGLY

It is the monitoring of performance relative to schedule that ultimately enabled Boeing to find out that its original delivery schedule was not realistic. To his credit, McNerney anticipated that there might be problems as far back as October 2006. And he had developed plans intended to keep the 787 program on track in the event that Boeing's monitoring of suppliers revealed problems. Back then McNerney said, "I would characterize what we are doing here as pretty aggressive contingency planning. We are at that point in the program where weight remains a dogged issue. We know what we have to do. Suppliers occasionally need help. And what I'm trying to do, along with the BCA team, is to put a contingency plan in place."[30]

According to McNerney, Boeing had eight contingency plans for the 787—one of which had been funded. This funded contingency plan pertained to "travel work"—work that is supposed to get done before the large composite fuselage barrels and wings of the 787 arrive in Everett, Washington, for final assembly of the planes. The *travel work* contingency plan was for Boeing machinists in Everett to complete the work that should have been done by the suppliers. The result was that Boeing would do the electrical wiring and systems installation travel work.[31]

McNerney was prudent to pay so much attention to contingency planning. Unfortunately, he did not anticipate all the problems that Boeing ultimately encountered. These problems included language barriers between Boeing and suppliers; the inability of suppliers to meet deadlines because they had subcontracted out work to suppliers who could not deliver on time; delay in building a fuselage factory in Italy because local regulators wanted to preserve an ancient olive grove; and the failure to anticipate and develop plans for a global shortage of fasteners needed to snap together the pieces of the aircraft. The first 787 to arrive at Boeing's factory was missing tens of thousands of parts. As the delays mounted, Boeing faced the prospect of paying billions of dollars in penalty payments to customers, as well as pressure from suppliers, many of which had agreed not to be paid until planes got delivered to customers.[32]

One of the worst problems emerged at Vought Aircraft Industries, Inc., a longtime Boeing supplier. Its job was to build the rear section of the fuselage. Vought retained design responsibility for the complicated carbon-fiber exterior, but it hired Israeli Aerospace Industries Ltd., of Tel Aviv, to design and build the section's floor. The task involved fabricating and assembling more than six thousand components, from lightweight beams to tiny brackets.

Problems arose in getting many of the items to conform to a tight set of engineering tolerances set by Boeing. Normally, this could have been addressed by taking each part through a review process involving a series of sign-offs that typically generate massive amounts of paperwork—approaching an inch-thick stack per part.

But Israeli Aerospace was halfway across the world and in the third rung of the new bureaucratic ladder. The sign-off process would have required each document to travel multiple times between Israel, Charleston, and Seattle. When it became apparent that this was threatening Vought's ability to deliver its fuselage section, teams of experts from Boeing and Vought were sent to Tel Aviv to walk each part through the process.[33]

Ultimately, due in part to reports he received from the field about these problems, McNerney decided to relieve Vought of some of its responsibilities. In March 2008, Boeing spent an undisclosed amount to buy Vought out of a joint venture with Italy's Alenia Aeronautica in South Carolina called Global Aeronautica (GA) after GA botched its assembly of the 787 fuselage at its South Carolina plant.[34] Vought continues to make the aft fuselage for the 787 at a plant adjacent to Global Aeronautica, while Boeing engineers will step in to oversee the preintegration.[35] According to McNerney, Boeing bought out GA "to relieve Vought of some of the pressure and get them focused."[36] While buying out a supplier is the most extreme example of how Boeing adjusted its supplier relationships based on monitoring suppliers' performance, McNerney has encouraged more subtle adjustments.

Such adjustments are important because if McNerney wants to succeed with outsourcing product development, Boeing's suppliers need to be able to do what they have promised. To that end, Boeing is shifting the preassembly work back to its suppliers. As Shanahan has said, "We thought we could modify our production system and accommodate the traveled work from our suppliers, and we were wrong. Our focus [now] is on not traveling the type of work that is disruptive to our production system." Boeing is trying to accomplish this by sending hundreds of its employees to its partners' factories in an effort to improve the work flow and reduce the stream of unfinished airplane sections to its Everett plant.[37]

The costs to Boeing and its customers of the gap between the original delivery schedule and the ultimate one are likely to reach into the billions of dollars. McNerney, of course, would have preferred to avoid them altogether. However, he remains determined to continue Boeing's approach of outsourcing the design and delivery of new aircraft components.

Ultimately, despite the delays, McNerney expects the benefits—

in the form of quicker time to market, shared financial risk, and better quality—to offset the financial and reputational damage to Boeing and to him. McNerney still believes that Boeing has a five-year advantage over Airbus, which is expected to begin delivering its midrange aircraft, the A350, in 2013.

And while he is optimistic about the outcome, he accepts some of the blame: "On the supply-chain side, I think we ran into some issues. We overestimated the ability of our partners to get things done with the timing we'd all hoped for. Our oversight of that environment was not as good as it could have been. It's a big global enterprise, this 787, and we have some problems that we've got to learn from, and we've got to do better. I don't think the guys in Seattle [where Boeing assembles the 787] would characterize me as low-profile regarding my involvement with the 787. Having said that, you can always look back on these situations and say if I'd moved two months earlier here or a month and a half earlier there . . . we probably could be in slightly better shape."[38]

CONCLUSION

McNerney's efforts to globalize product development at Boeing are likely to pay off in the long run. They provide many potential benefits, including obtaining the services of the world's most capable engineering and manufacturing talent in applying new technologies, shifting risk from Boeing to its suppliers, and accelerating time to market. McNerney's objectives were ambitious, and in seeking to achieve them, he ran into problems. He has learned that he can prevent these problems from recurring by restoring trust up and down the line and with Boeing's suppliers. And he has shifted from a **delegate-and-trust** approach *to* a **trust-but-verify** one.

CHAPTER 10.

MAKE ETHICS AND COMPLIANCE A CLEAR COMPETITIVE ADVANTAGE

A series of ethical problems at Boeing helped propel Jim Mc-Nerney into the CEO's job. In the two years before he was hired, as we'll explore further below it was revealed that the company had coddled an employee, Kenneth Branch, who had stolen documents from a competitor and that it had improperly offered a job to a government procurement officer Darleen Druyun. Then the CEO who was brought in to clean up the mess had an affair with a subordinate and was forced to resign.

McNerney's predecessors had shredded Boeing's reputation, and the company had a culture that appeared to put more value on winning contracts and making money than on ethical behavior. One of the board's primary reasons for selecting McNerney was his own reputation for straight-shooting honesty. Jim McNerney was known for having clear moral standards, for sticking to them, and for embedding them in the organizations he led. His first assignment at Boeing was to resolve the legal problems resulting from the procurement and document scandals and to make sure that in the future no such problems would recur.

Those scandals were not minor; they were huge. As Boeing's general counsel Doug Bain pointed out at a January 2006 Orlando,

Florida, leadership retreat, the cost of its ethical blindness was very high. Bain asked the 260 Boeing executives, "Was there a culture of win at any cost? We now know what that cost is."[1] The scandals included inducing an air force procurement officer to grant a big contract to Boeing in exchange for employment offers for her family; inappropriate use of a competitor's intellectual property; and violation of export laws.

In order to repair the damage from these scandals, McNerney acted on three fronts. He settled a series of lawsuits against Boeing, decided not to take a tax deduction for the settlement payment, and testified in front of Congress. Here are the key points of each:

- **Settlement.** McNerney put these problems behind Boeing. According to the *New York Times*, "The $615 million settlement ended a three-year investigation and allowed Boeing to avoid criminal charges over accusations that it had improperly acquired proprietary documents from a rival, Lockheed Martin, and had illegally recruited an Air Force weapons buyer who was overseeing Boeing contracts.[2]

- **No tax deduction.** McNerney forced Boeing shareholders to pay a short-term price for restoring public trust in Boeing when in July 2006, it announced that it would not seek a tax deduction for the $615 million it had paid to the government—a decision that McNerney said would cost $200 million.

- **Congressional testimony.** And the next month, McNerney found himself in front of Congress trying to draw a line in the sand between his tenure and that of his predecessors. During August 2006 testimony, McNerney said, "I hope to discuss why, going forward, the Congress and the taxpayers of this country can place their trust in Boeing. Companies doing business with the U.S. government are expected to adhere to the highest legal and ethical standards. I acknowledge that Boeing did not live up to those expectations."[3]

To understand how McNerney accomplished this change, it's useful to know more about his character. While McNerney's character was shaped long before he arrived at GE and Boeing, he clearly demonstrated an intuitive sense of "right action" in both companies. McNerney demonstrated his ethical values by living them, not by preaching about them. According to the retired GE executive, "He influenced people by his integrity and morals. When you get to know somebody real well you see behind the curtain—whether there are any gray areas. He didn't have gray areas. He knew what to do intuitively."[4]

At GE, he was willing to put the customer's interests above GE's short-term financial calculations. For example, when a customer had a technical problem with an aircraft engine, McNerney would fix it even though the fine print of the warranty may have let GE off the hook for the repair. And at Boeing, he was able to make significant progress in fixing its ethically challenged culture through a rich mixture of leadership style, organizational changes, and process.

At GE, McNerney demonstrated in many ways the strength of his ethical compass. Two specific stories illustrate McNerney's strong sense of right and wrong:

- **Put 3M's interests above his career goals.** McNerney had a long-standing desire to run Boeing, an ambition that he put on hold when Boeing came calling the first time because he believed he still had an unfulfilled commitment to 3M. According to a retired GE executive, "Jim was always going to go to Boeing. He said, 'If there's any job I want, it's to run Boeing.' But when he left GE, the Boeing job wasn't open. So he went to 3M. When Condit left Boeing, the board went to McNerney and said, 'Jim, we'd like you to take over and run Boeing.' But Jim said, 'I haven't finished what I started to do. I'm not going to take it.' He made the decision on principle and later regretted it. He said to himself, 'This may never happen again.' " Still, when Stonecipher left, McNerney initially took himself out of the running again. "Finally, when they asked him again, he thought, 'This isn't going to come again.' And he accepted the offer. He felt that he had finished what he needed at 3M."[5]

- **Put customer's interests first.** McNerney's integrity carried over to doing what was right for a customer over the longer term, even though it might lead to short-term costs for GE that might not be strictly required by a contract. According to the retired GE executive, "Jim would see into the longer-term future. If an airline has a problem with an engine, it is going to be a concern to the FAA. It can become a huge problem in the industry. There is pressure from the aircraft manufacturer to fix the problem. Things get tense. Jim responds, 'You're right, and I'm going to fix this. If it doesn't fit the warranty, we're still going to fix this.' Jim would see beyond the dollars and cents. Customers will appreciate it. Jim is not up for sainthood. But he's good."[6]

McNerney brought this ethical compass to Boeing to transform its culture into one with a focus on ethics. Here are six steps McNerney is taking to accomplish the transformation:

- He directly addresses the sources of ethical problems in company culture
- He adds ethical conduct to explicit values
- He requires leaders to model ethical behavior

- He opens channels to discuss ethical and business problems
- He links promotion and pay to ethical conduct
- He looks for ethics problems, doesn't wait for them to surface

HE DIRECTLY ADDRESSES THE SOURCES OF ETHICAL PROBLEMS IN COMPANY CULTURE

McNerney takes the approach of a consultant seeking to diagnose the problems. At Boeing, he started by asking probing questions about how Boeing's culture produced so many ethical problems. The questions included:

- Are these lapses symptomatic of a larger issue within Boeing's corporate culture?
- Does Boeing lack the systems and processes to guide its people toward ethical behavior?
- Do Boeing's leaders model ethical behavior, and do they routinely discuss ethical issues with their teams?
- Do Boeing's people feel confident enough to speak up about ethical concerns without fear of retaliation?
- Do Boeing employees hide in the bureaucracy; do they wink at wrongdoing or look the other way?
- Do Boeing investigative units and oversight bodies talk to one another, or do they operate in isolation from one another?[7]

Through these questions, McNerney pinpointed the weaknesses in Boeing's culture. Specifically, he found that while a few individuals chose not to follow the proper processes, certain cultural weaknesses had permitted people who suspected a problem, including Boeing's leadership, to look the other way.[8] McNerney realized that if he could not find a way to make his findings compelling to Boeing's executives, things would not change. He concluded that a dramatic gesture would grab the attention of Boeing's leaders far more effectively than a dull diatribe from him.

To stage this drama, McNerney used the forum of the Orlando leadership retreat. And rather than deliver this gesture himself, McNerney put the burden on Bain, who delivered a devastating worst-case assessment of the potential damage that still loomed from Boeing's then-recent ethics scandals. Bain's speech also offered insight into how Boeing hoped to recover from the scandals, retrieve its reputation, and ensure ethical behavior in the future.[9]

Bain highlighted the penalties that faced Boeing because of the two major defense scandals and for alleged breaches of export laws. He noted that Boeing faced potential indictment by U.S. attorneys on the East and West coasts, and that the Department of Justice estimated that the damages facing Boeing exceeded $5 billion. Furthermore, Bain noted that Boeing could be barred from government contracts or denied export licenses for both military and commercial sales.[10]

Here was Bain's list of Boeing's ethical lowlights: *Slide*

- **Executive departures.** An "astronomically high" fifteen company vice presidents had been pushed out of Boeing for various ethical lapses in recent years. Among them was Chief Financial Officer Mike Sears, who in 2002 offered a job to Darleen Druyun, chief acquisitions officer at the air force, while she was overseeing work on Boeing contracts. At her sentencing hearing in 2004, Druyun said she favored Boeing on multiple contracts because of favors granted by the company, including hiring her daughter and son-in-law. The scandal sent Sears and Druyun to jail, forced the resignation of then-CEO Phil Condit, and jeopardized major defense contracts, including the air force tanker program, which would have secured up to eight thousand jobs in Everett, Washington.[11]

- **Unauthorized use of proprietary documents.** In 1997, Mc-Donnell Douglas hired a manager away from Lockheed Martin to work on the Delta IV rocket program. He brought with him proprietary documents, including financial details on Lockheed's planned bid for an air force space rocket competition. Boeing merged with McDonnell Douglas later that year. After the documents were discovered, three Boeing employees were indicted. The Pentagon stripped Boeing of seven rocket launches and suspended Boeing's rocket division from new government business for twenty months.[12]

- **Looking the other way.** Who was this manager, and what exactly did he and Boeing do wrong? Kenneth Branch was the Lockheed Martin manager who accepted a job in 1997 with McDonnell Douglas in its space rocket program, which later became a Boeing unit competing against Lockheed. Branch took about twenty-five thousand pages of documents, many with proprietary markings, from Lockheed Martin. About a dozen Boeing employees saw some of these documents over two and a half years. It was only in June 1999 that an employee came forward. "How could you have that many documents floating around and nobody said anything?" Bain asked at his presentation in Orlando.[13]

- **Violating export laws.** Boeing also violated export laws. Between 2000 and 2003, Boeing exported commercial jets with a QRS-11 gyrochip in the instrument flight boxes, even though the chip was classified by the State Department as an export-restricted defense item because it can be used to stabilize and steer guided missiles. In 2005, the State Department prepared civil charges alleging ninety-four violations of the Arms Control Act. Boeing faced a potential fine of as much as $47 million.[14]

- **Jailed executives.** Boeing's ethical transgressions cost two executives their freedom. Bain noted that his talk reflected "the perspective of the prosecutors and what they have told us," rather than Boeing's position on the legal issues. And he decided to scare his executive audience straight. In so doing, he rattled off the federal prisoner numbers of Druyun and Sears—noting "these are not ZIP codes." He exhorted his audience to change, noting, "Our job as the leaders of this enterprise is to establish a culture that ensures there is no next time. The bottom line is we just cannot stand another major scandal."[15]

Within Boeing, the number of ethics cases was extraordinarily high. Bain pointed out that nine hundred of the formal ethics cases brought by employees to Boeing's Office of Ethics and Business Conduct in 2005 were found to have substance. Moreover, he cited an employee survey in which 26 percent of those surveyed said they had observed abusive or intimidating behavior by management. And of the fifteen Boeing vice presidents terminated for ethics violations in recent years, Bain said two had been fired for committing crimes and the rest for offenses ranging from expense-account fraud to sexual harassment.[16]

McNerney's dramatic presentation of Boeing's ethical flaws, via Bain, was designed to create a sense of urgency. Executives had to realize that the continued success of the company and of their careers was at stake. They had to change their behavior and do it quickly.

HE ADDS ETHICAL CONDUCT
TO EXPLICIT VALUES

As he created a sense of urgency, McNerney crafted explicit values for Boeing—many of which were identical to the ones he had defined at 3M. Among the values that he articulated for Boeing was the emphasis on ethical conduct. Like his predecessor, Harry Stonecipher, McNerney required each employee to sign Boeing's code of conduct and to take annual ethics training. However, Mc-Nerney, unlike Stonecipher, made it clear that he expected Boeing's people to commit themselves to ethics on a piece of paper **and** to *behave* ethically. While Stonecipher viewed ethics as an annual pro forma exercise, McNerney viewed it as an ongoing process.

McNerney realized early on that unethical behavior permeated Boeing. The fact that the scandals involved misconduct in a number of geographic locations and in nearly every Boeing division made it clear to him that Boeing had a toxic culture. Or, as McNerney politely put it, "I think the culture had morphed in dysfunctional ways in some places. There are elements of our culture that I think we all would like to change. If we can get the values lined up with performance, then this is an absolutely unbeatable company."[17]

One way that McNerney hoped to add ethical conduct to Boeing's culture was through leadership development. As McNerney said, "I plan to make leadership development a focus across the company because I believe that as we strengthen our leadership capacities, we can have a positive impact on the company's overall performance. As I've said before, better leaders make better companies. And effective leadership, at all levels of an organization, is based on a foundation of trust, integrity and escape-free compliance. As we turn up the gain in leadership-development training, we will embed in it an equal emphasis on how leaders can lead with ethics and integrity."[18]

As McNerney has done in all the cultural change initiatives he's led, he moves from an initial emphasis on changing values and leadership development to putting *teeth* into the values. If people initially think McNerney's values are a passing fad, they soon discover that he is quite serious about them. If they have not been behaving in a way that's consistent with Boeing's values, he expects them to change their behavior. And if they don't meet McNerney's expectations, they lose their leadership roles.

HE REQUIRES LEADERS TO MODEL ETHICAL BEHAVIOR

McNerney recognizes the critical importance of leaders' influence over their people. He knows that if leaders act ethically, then the people who report to them will have to follow suit. Conversely, if Boeing's leaders don't act ethically, then the rest of the organization is likely to behave unethically. The failure of McNerney's predecessors to model ethical behavior almost certainly contributed to the widespread problems that Boeing faced.

McNerney knew that the obligation to model ethical behavior began with him. And he modeled ethical behavior when he testified in front of Congress in August 2006 after Boeing settled the charges that Bain had outlined at the Orlando meeting. During McNerney's testimony before the Senate Armed Services Committee, he told members that as part of Boeing's ethics and compliance program, all employees must sign Boeing's code of conduct annually and participate in yearly ethics recommitment sessions. McNerney also described Boeing's creation of the Office of Internal Governance (OIG), which monitors and tracks potential conflicts of interest in hiring and provides oversight of ethics and compliance concerns for Boeing's top leaders.[19]

McNerney suggested that Boeing's ethics and compliance efforts were the "silver lining of this dark cloud in our history." But more than just creating an ethics program, McNerney has succeeded in steering Boeing clear of ethics controversy and lessening

the scandalous taint that surrounded it under Condit and Stonecipher. According to Peter Jacobs, an analyst for Ragen MacKenzie
in Seattle, Washington, "At the [end of his first year as Boeing's
CEO], Jim McNerney's contribution has mainly been in returning credibility to the corporate office. He has raised the ethical bar
and put into place things to prevent some of the misdeeds of the
past."[20]

McNerney also modeled ethical behavior in the way he resolved the three-year Justice Department investigation into defense contracting scandals. The final settlement, announced in
May 2006, required Boeing to pay the government $615
million—the largest financial penalty a military contractor has
ever incurred without having to face criminal charges or admit
wrongdoing. The settlement put an end to two matters facing
Boeing—the stolen Lockheed Martin documents and the Sears/
Druyun legal entanglements.

When Boeing announced its earnings in July 2006, McNerney decided not to take advantage of a provision that could have
saved it $200 million in taxes by writing off the settlement pay-
ment against its earnings. Since the announcement came weeks
before McNerney was scheduled to testify before Senators Charles
Grassley, John Warner, and John McCain, the decision helped de-
fuse suspicion within Congress that Boeing had gotten off too
lightly. In the view of Aboulafia, "It's better to eat the cost and not
make yourself a target. This was a savvy move."[21]

McNerney decided not to take the tax write-off for a deeper
reason. According to the retired GE executive, "Jim was urged by
Boeing's lawyers to take the write-off. But his internal compass
told him that it was simply not the right thing to do. It was because of his own sense of what was right and wrong that he decided not to use the penalty to reduce Boeing's taxes."[22] Perhaps,
as Aboulafia suggests, the decision was also intended to keep Boeing from raising hackles in Congress.

McNerney also used this decision to send a message to Wall Street and Boeing's employees. As he said in a July 26, 2006, conference call, "Without question, the short-term financial impact of the taxability issue is significant. However, the long-term value of Boeing's reputation is even more significant. This should be a signal to our employees, customers, suppliers, and our shareholders of our willingness to acknowledge responsibility and to accept accountability and to move forward. Simply speaking, my intent is to focus on the future and put this unfortunate part of our past behind us."[23]

McNerney spoke with Boeing's leaders to make it clear to them how important it was for them to behave ethically and to expect ethical behavior from others. As McNerney said, "We also realize it all starts with leadership. If an organization's leaders don't model, encourage, expect and reward the right behaviors, why should anyone else in that organization exhibit those behaviors? Companies have to take the hugely important step of driving ethics and compliance through their core leadership and Human Resources processes. This must be . . . and must be seen to be . . . a central part of the whole system of training and developing leaders and of the whole process of evaluating and promoting people. This is the key."[24]

McNerney clearly saw the potential to make Boeing better than its competitors by changing its culture. And he would measure the success of the change by observing whether its leaders were excited and empowered. As he argued, "At the end of the day, the ethos or character of an organization . . . its culture . . . comes down to the behavior of its leaders; leaders get the behavior they exhibit and tolerate. What really makes the difference between one company and another? More than anything else, it's people and how they view themselves and their jobs. Are they excited about what they do? Do they feel empowered? Do they feel they can speak their mind freely . . . or do they have to be wheedled and cajoled into giving an opinion? You can always tell if you go out among your people and are willing to listen."[25] The ones who perform better are almost always the ones who are excited and empowered.

McNerney's expectations that leaders should behave ethically suggests four lessons for leaders. To encourage ethical behavior, the CEO must:

- Act ethically—and do so in a very public way;
- Communicate the expectation that the company's top leaders will behave ethically;
- Promote leaders who meet these expectations and sideline those who don't; and
- Encourage leaders to do the same for the people they manage.

HE OPENS CHANNELS TO DISCUSS ETHICAL AND BUSINESS PROBLEMS

One of the behaviors that McNerney modeled was encouraging Boeing's people to talk about ethical and business problems. By opening up the flow of information from employees to management, McNerney let Boeing's people know that he wanted them to discuss problems and not bury them. Part of McNerney's diagnosis of Boeing's cultural problems was that its instincts were not to discuss problems and that this would ultimately make moot all his efforts to encourage ethical action.

So McNerney confronted that environment by encouraging people to talk about difficult ethics-related issues. He did this himself when meeting with groups of fifty to seventy-five employees around Boeing. As he said, "I make ethics and compliance a regular topic of conversation. If they don't bring it up, I do. We talk about it. The dialogue is rich, and openness and candor are a big part of it."[26]

McNerney also encourages all Boeing's leaders to engage in conversations about ethics and compliance with their people. Ultimately, McNerney wants to avoid surprises about ethical problems that originate at lower levels. He wants to create a culture where leaders will not tolerate or encourage unethical behavior. As McNerney said, "I'm not the only one who does this. I expect all of the leaders at Boeing, from front-line supervisors to the top leaders of our company, to talk with their teams about ethics and compliance. I don't mean 'preaching,' but initiating an open and probing dialogue and doing their level best to unearth problems and concerns."[27]

McNerney made it clear to Boeing that he wanted to create a culture where people felt comfortable discussing ethical problems. Moreover, he wants Boeing people to pursue profit and to behave ethically. He views the two as mutually reinforcing activities. And in a not-so-subtle way, he was trying to make a break from his predecessors, who seemed to think that unethical behavior in the pursuit of profit was tolerable. As McNerney said, "I know . . . and you know . . . that one of the absolute prerequisites for success in ethics and compliance is the belief that it is OK for people to question what happens around them."[28]

And he urged Boeing's people to understand that questioning unethical behavior should not be seen as threatening to them or to the business. McNerney argued, "There shouldn't be an either-or consideration here. Something done unethically hurts our ability to perform. We are in a business. A business must make a profit to continue operating. The only way to make a profit and to operate long-term is to conduct our work ethically and compliantly. You should speak up if you're aware of something wrong. Boeing offers a broad array of resources to help people make ethical decisions and to report possible violations. Please use these resources. You'll be doing our company a favor, and you'll be doing the right thing."[29]

McNerney sought to change Boeing's culture from one that tolerated unethical acts in pursuit of profit to one that saw ethics as a way to sustain profit growth. In making that change, McNerney's actions suggest the following lessons for leaders:

- Initiate a dialogue with people about ethics and compliance issues.
- Encourage people to discuss behavior that may cross the ethical line.
- Monitor how well leaders are spurring the flow of such discussions.
- Encourage leaders to do the same for the people they manage.

HE LINKS PROMOTIONS AND PAY
TO ETHICAL CONDUCT

McNerney used Boeing's human resources systems—those processes that train people, evaluate their performance, and determine their career paths, pay, and bonuses—to link people's ambitions to ethical conduct. By doing this, McNerney pulled Boeing's people toward the idea that he would reward them for getting results ethically. And conversely, if he saw unethical conduct he would push them out the door. These clear messages helped to change behavior throughout Boeing.

One thing he did differently was to link pay and bonuses to how well executives embrace "Boeing values." Under Stonecipher and Condit, no points were awarded for collaborating with other units or following ethics rules. Under McNerney, pay and promotions are directly linked to how well executives model Boeing's values—including ethics. As he told Congress, "We have begun to measure and factor into the whole pay and promotion process [ethical] behavior [and if it's not simple, you can't measure it]. We are doing this partly through 360-degree evaluations[30] of our leaders at all levels—asking how well they do in modeling each of the six leadership attributes." One of these attributes is "Live the Boeing Values," which, among other things, include promoting integrity and avoiding abusive behavior."[31]

McNerney also made it clear that he would take away the jobs of leaders who don't measure up. As he said, "And frankly speaking, if certain people are only able to measure up well on 'delivers results,' [and not on the values part] they will soon find that they have no future with Boeing. In short, we are molding the kind of leadership that we want to take into the future. And part of that is getting rid of abusive leaders and anyone who thinks it is better to lead through fear and intimidation than it is through the ability to include and inspire people."[32]

McNerney changed Boeing's process for evaluating, promoting, and paying people to encourage them to behave ethically. The way he did this suggests four lessons for leaders:

- Make ethical values part of performance evaluation.
- Use 360-degree reviews to encourage employees, peers, and bosses to assess their ethical conduct.
- Get rid of leaders who don't measure up.
- Reward those who do.

HE LOOKS FOR ETHICS PROBLEMS, DOESN'T WAIT FOR THEM TO SURFACE

In searching for answers to his questions, McNerney pinpointed the weaknesses in Boeing's culture. One of the things he found was that while some individuals chose not to follow the proper processes, certain cultural weaknesses had permitted other people, including Boeing's leadership, who suspected a problem, to look the other way. McNerney believed that he needed to set up a formal system to monitor and look for violations. In the Office of Internal Governance (OIG), he set up a centralized ethics and compliance unit. Among its responsibilities was establishing a data-mining system to enable Boeing's business leaders to detect potential ethical misconduct and take corrective actions to avoid serious mistakes.[33]

The OIG, which reports to McNerney and Boeing's board, helps Boeing identify ethical concerns before they reach a crisis and bring those concerns to Boeing's top executives fast with enough data to be able to take appropriate action. According to McNerney, OIG has three responsibilities:

- "**Acting** as a strong check and balance for key functional disciplines. An example would be monitoring and tracking such things as potential conflicts of interest through our hiring, transfer and proposal process.
- **Providing** significantly greater visibility into—and oversight of—specific ethics and compliance concerns and cases for our top leaders.
- **Consolidating,** in one organization, our various investigative, audit and oversight sources. This way, we are able to identify potential problems earlier and take corrective action earlier."[34]

By sharing information across different departments, including compliance, law, and human resources, OIG is able to pinpoint problems before they develop very far. An office like OIG alone would not be enough to encourage ethical behavior at Boeing. But when used in conjunction with individual ethics training and a culture that rewards ethical behavior, OIG has been effective in McNerney's efforts to change Boeing's culture.

CONCLUSION

Jim McNerney has transformed Boeing's culture into one that places a premium on ethical behavior. The way he did it suggests five behaviors for leaders seeking to do the same:

- **Send a signal that the CEO will lead ethics and compliance.** McNerney's leadership on ethics and compliance was in clear contrast to the role of Condit and Stonecipher. By personally taking on this leadership role, McNerney meant to signal to Boeing's customers, regulators, board, employees, and investors that he would put his own reputation on the line to keep Boeing out of ethics and compliance trouble.
- **Demand that top executives model ethical and compliant behavior.** McNerney made it clear that executives needed to behave ethically and in compliance with Boeing values and with relevant laws and regulations. This imperative had two practical benefits. First, such behavior diminished the chance that employees would be asked to do something unethical or illegal by their boss. Second, such behavior would show ambitious employees that ethics and compliance could be a means of getting ahead in the organization.
- **Clarify the importance of getting results the right way.** McNerney also made it clear through his role in setting Boeing's values and teaching them at its training center that ethics and compliance were a critical part of everyone's job. He reinforced the importance of this idea by making it clear that anyone who achieved business results while violating principles of

ethics and compliance would "have no future at Boeing." This statement, when backed by personnel changes, sent a powerful message to Boeing's people.

- **Create an independent unit to monitor ethics and compliance.** While McNerney wanted each individual to have a clear internal compass and rewarded those who followed that compass, he did not believe this was sufficient. That's why he created the six-hundred-person OIG to make sure that people within Boeing were acting within ethical and compliance guidelines. Through OIG, McNerney wanted to assure that when problems arose, Boeing would uncover them and deal with them quickly.

- **Create a competitive advantage.** Finally, by setting the goal of making ethics and compliance a clear competitive advantage at Boeing, McNerney sent a signal that he believed that ethics and compliance could contribute to superior business results. He made it clear that ethics and compliance were not window dressing but a way to lower Boeing's costs and increase its revenues. To the extent that Boeing succeeds in implementing this principle, its shareholders, its employees, the communities where it works, and everyone it touches around the world will benefit.

CHAPTER 11.

CUT YOUR COMPANY'S ENVIRONMENTAL FOOTPRINT

As we've seen throughout this book, Jim McNerney combines an instinct to do the right thing with a desire to win. And these two streams of his personality intersect powerfully when it comes to Boeing's strategy toward the environment. His instinct to do the right thing has created a great sense of urgency when it comes to taking action to reduce the air and noise pollution that the aircraft industry generates. But as CEO, McNerney must combine his instinct to do right with his obligation to boost Boeing's economic value.

This raises a key question: Are concerns about a company's environmental impact mere marketing sheen or is there a good business reason to cut a company's environmental emissions? The answer probably varies company to company. However, in the case of Boeing, there are fundamental reasons why reducing its environmental footprint makes business sense. Unlike the United States, European leaders take matters of global warming and noise pollution quite seriously. European environmental regulators measure environmental pollution and pursue policies to reduce it.

This matters to Boeing for at least two reasons. First, Boeing sells to airlines based in Europe, and those airlines are increasingly interested in buying aircraft that produce lower carbon emissions. As we saw in chapter 5, Boeing's European competitor Airbus chose to build the 450-seat, gas-guzzling A380, which puts it at a competitive disadvantage to Boeing's 787 in the minds of those environmentally conscious European airline customers. Second, if Boeing wants to continue to sell in Europe, it must take an especially cautious approach because all things being equal, European customers would prefer to buy from Airbus than from an American company. And by responding to the environmental concerns of European politicians and regulators, Boeing can take advantage of Airbus's competitive weakness.

A competitive strategy based on reducing a company's environmental footprint changes how it operates. This transformation, as does any deep corporate change, starts with the CEO. McNerney kicked off his change campaign with the belief that companies must consider the environment in all elements of their business and operating plan. Boeing recently elevated its environmental team higher in its organization chart. And Boeing's new products generate less noise and fewer produce emissions.

Boeing plans to sustain the lower environmental footprints of its products by using composite materials in at least half of the structural components of new jets. The composites are made of nonmetallic fibers—carbon, fiberglass, or aramid (a flame-resistant, cut-proof material)—embedded in a resin of plastic or epoxy. They are stronger than aluminum but weigh half as much. Lighter planes consume less fuel and cost airlines less in airport landing fees. Additionally, composite jets could go as much as twice as long between maintenance events—saving the airlines even more money. Nevertheless, while the airline industry generates what it considers a relatively small share of total air pollution, McNerney believes that Boeing has a responsibility to lead the industry in reducing that share.[1]

McNerney does many things to cut Boeing's environmental footprint.

- He pushes Boeing to reduce carbon and noise levels.
- He builds products with smaller environmental footprints.
- He wins customers who value such products.
- He works with governments to encourage more stringent environmental regulation.
- He boosts the role of Boeing's environmental strategy department.

HE PUSHES BOEING TO REDUCE CARBON AND NOISE LEVELS

McNerney believes that Boeing should lead rather than resist pressure to reduce its environmental footprint—i.e., the level of carbon and noise that it emits through the production and operation of aircraft. In so doing, he is responding to pressure from Europe, whose citizens are strongly concerned about cleaning up the environment. McNerney's response is both the right thing to do socially and a smart business strategy. As he has said, "I think the environment really has to be built into all elements of your business and operating plan today. It is a big deal and it should be a big deal. This is not a company that resists the idea. This is a company that wants to be part of a solution."[2]

McNerney has also made it clear that he sees a greater sense of urgency about environmental concerns coming from Europe than from the United States. Influential global citizens—such as former vice president Al Gore who won a Nobel Prize for his documentary film, *An Inconvenient Truth*—also contribute to the need to act. Such pressure makes politicians and regulators feel that they must appear to be doing something to improve the environment. And this desire to act represents a business opportunity for companies such as Boeing. As McNerney says, "The European sensitivity has obviously outrun the U.S., but I think the U.S. is not far behind. It's not only a regulatory issue. It's a grass roots issue. You see everybody from ex–vice presidents to movie-makers becoming involved."[3]

However, McNerney has made it clear that he wants Boeing to do something about the problem by reducing the environmental footprint of its products. The way to do that is to change the way Boeing designs, builds, manufactures, and operates its products. This means designing aircraft that use less energy to build and operate and also generate less chemical pollution and noise when airlines fly them. As McNerney says, "The things that we focus on are number one, our products. There are those in our industry that feel we are picked on because we only generate 2 percent of carbon dioxide [CO_2] emissions and 2 percent of nitrous oxide [NOX] emissions. That's still a big number. We have to work on it."[4]

As we've seen throughout this book, McNerney believes that the CEO has a powerful role in setting high expectations for people and rewarding those who meet those expectations. McNerney uses this power at Boeing to change people's behavior. But he does more than simply talk about reducing Boeing's environmental footprint and expect people to figure out how to achieve that reduction. He leads specific initiatives—such as using technology to reduce the environmental footprints of Boeing's products—which he believes are critical to achieving his goals.

HE BUILDS PRODUCTS WITH SMALLER ENVIRONMENTAL FOOTPRINTS

McNerney is pushing Boeing to build products that pollute less. In so doing, he adapts to the interests of Boeing's communities—

specifically politicians, regulators, airlines, and airline passengers—who want cleaner, quieter aircraft operating in their jurisdictions. McNerney cites the 787 as an example of how Boeing is working to reduce the environmental impact of its products in response to what airline regulators want—less air pollution. As McNerney says, "The 787 is a very good example of what we are doing. The footprint is significantly less—noise is in the range of 30 percent to 40 percent lower and emissions are down 25 percent."[5]

But the 787 is a product that is well on its way to being delivered. How is McNerney putting his environmentally friendly product strategy into effect for Boeing's new products? One way is to reduce the environmental footprint of its replacement for the narrow-body 737. As we saw in chapter 4, an important part of achieving such design goals is incorporating new technologies that benefit customers. And in building the replacement for Boeing's 737, McNerney wants to choose materials and set engine design standards that reduce air and noise pollution. McNerney argues, "As we begin to think about the narrow-body replacement, we're already thinking today [that] it has to be an environmental step-function change. That will guide the materials we use and how we work with the engine manufacturers."[6]

He clearly wanted Boeing and its partners to reduce the environmental impact of an aircraft. And a big part of his role as CEO was to encourage technical choices—such as which material to use for an airframe—that would reduce the aircraft's environmental footprint. McNerney believed that using composite materials instead of aluminum in the fuselage of the 737 replacement would reduce by significant amounts its energy consumption and carbon emissions. As he said, "I think the introduction of composites have raised the ability of the airframe to make a difference, to provide more of a step-function opportunity, and really puts it on par with the engine development. I think when aluminum use plateaued, the engine probably made a bigger difference, and now it's more equally shared. Both have to happen. We need to have a step-function in engines, and we need to have some form of new materials—probably carbon-based—for the fuselage."[7]

Boeing veterans believe that McNerney has placed a renewed emphasis on reducing the company's environmental footprint. While Boeing has long been concerned about reducing the environmental footprint of its products, McNerney is its first CEO to see the competitive advantages of such concerns. For example, Carson suggests that Boeing had a long history of progress in reducing the environmental footprint of its products but had not made the general public aware of the progress. According to Carson, "Our track record is strong: over the last 40 years the industry has reduced noise footprints by 90 percent and specific CO_2 emissions by 70 percent; we have virtually eliminated hydrocarbon emissions and soot. And yet we have failed to communicate this message effectively and must better capitalize on our communications. Technology is the key that will allow Boeing to achieve a 25 percent efficiency improvement in worldwide fleet fuel use and CO_2 emissions by 2020 by enabling us to introduce more efficient products, make improvements to the current fleet and ameliorate carrier and airport operations."[8]

While Carson points out that Boeing is making significant environmental progress on its 787, he also suggests that Boeing is investing in R&D to reduce the future environmental footprint of its products yet to be developed. Specifically, Boeing is conducting research to cut air and noise pollution and to use non-fossil-based fuels. As Carson says, "BCA's R&D department is engaged in research in the areas of CO_2 and noise reduction, and alternatives to fossil fuels. The first bio-fuel demonstration flights, in collaboration with our partners, are scheduled for 2008."[9]

One of the most fascinating areas in which Boeing is at work to achieve a smaller environmental footprint is its research on fuel cell technology. José Enrique Roman, a manager at Boeing Research and Technology Europe, presented his work on Boeing's Fuel Cell Demonstrator Airplane project at a forum in December 2007. This project used an energy source derived from oxygen and hydrogen to produce the electrical energy needed to power an aircraft. Roman's technology is more efficient than a traditional internal combustion engine and produces no carbon emissions because it does not use fossil fuel. As Roman said, "Fuel cells are electro-chemical devices which use oxygen and hydrogen to produce electricity and water in a way that can be twice as efficient as a combustion engine and use no fossil fuels. This project has been in progress since 2003 with several European partners from Austria, France, Germany, Spain and the United Kingdom. The first ground tests have just been successfully completed and we are working with the Spanish aviation authority to obtain the first experimental flight permit as soon as possible."[10]

Boeing is also working on a way for aircraft to burn less fuel as they land. This procedure, called continuous descent arrival (CDA), promised more fuel-efficient aircraft. While airlines use CDA when airport traffic is relatively low, Boeing is working on ways to adapt CDA so that airlines can use it when there is more traffic and/or weather conditions are less favorable. As Roman pointed out, "Today, conventional approach operations are carried out in steps, which increases the engine thrust and therefore fuel burn and noise. CDA's environmental benefits are huge and the technique is already used in some airports, at night or when traffic is not dense. But because of wind uncertainty it does not procure optimal landing predictability for air traffic controllers and therefore has repercussions on airport capacity."[11]

Roman continued by pointing out the specific goals of Boeing's CDA research. He noted, "We are working on CDA for maximum predictability by establishing a new vertical guidance law. By modifying current practices predictability differentials could be reduced from 30 seconds to three seconds, which would mean that CDA could be used in denser traffic. Once this law has been proved we will progress to test flights."[12]

The most critical prong of McNerney's strategy to reduce Boeing's environmental footprint is to invest in products that pollute less. McNerney does this by placing bets on existing technologies—such as composites—and by wagering R&D on non-carbon-based sources of power and new ways to fly aircraft so that they burn less fuel and make less noise as they land. McNerney's comprehensive approach reflects the high value he places on the goal of reducing Boeing's environmental footprint.

HE WINS CUSTOMERS WHO VALUE
SUCH PRODUCTS

Is all this environmentally friendly investment in aircraft technology just a feel-good exercise, or does it have some payoff for Boeing shareholders? The simple answer is that in many cases it is too early to tell. That's because so many of these investments will not pay off in the short term. However, at least one airline decided to buy aircraft from Boeing because of their environmental advantages over the products they will replace. This example suggests that Boeing shareholders could earn rich payoffs from McNerney's investment in reducing the environmental footprint of its products.

The customer was British entrepreneur Richard Branson's Virgin Airlines. In April 2007, Boeing's focus on reducing the environmental impact of its products paid off when Virgin bought fifteen 787s with options on eight more. The order was worth $2.8 billion at list prices and about $1.8 billion with standard discounts.[13]

Branson said that he bought the 787 because of its relatively small environmental footprint and its relatively early delivery date. Branson concluded that the 787—made from 50 percent composite materials—would be 27 percent more fuel efficient and 60 percent less noisy than the Airbus A340 jet that it would replace. Moreover, the 787's two engines would create a big environmental advantage because the rest of the Virgin fleet had four. Furthermore, although Airbus promised even bigger fuel savings—and hence lower carbon emissions—with its A350, that aircraft was not anticipated to enter service until 2013 at the earliest.[14] Thus, the 787's time-to-market advantage, which we discussed in chapter 9, when combined with its smaller environmental footprint, helped Boeing to win a big order from Virgin.

But this was not the only payoff Boeing anticipated from its efforts to reduce its environmental footprint. Virgin also joined with Boeing and its engine manufacturer, GE, to develop a new generation of biofuels to power future aircraft—a move that could cut Virgin's carbon footprint dramatically. The goal of this partnership was to demonstrate the technology on a Boeing 747 jumbo in 2008. McNerney points out that the partnership was considering several types of biofuel for this demonstration. As he says, the possibilities include fuel "from Soya beans and algae to grain and 'cellulosic' crops such as prairie grass. Until now, it had not been thought feasible to produce eco-friendly aviation fuel, because conventional fuels such as ethanol freeze at altitudes higher than 15,000 feet." Aboulafia says airlines are tired of flying planes that are not as fuel-efficient as the 787. As he points out, "I can't help but think there is an arms race going on, an airline economic arms race. If your competitor has a plane that is 20 percent more fuel-efficient, you can either match them or watch your profits get wiped out."[15]

In responding more aggressively to the objectives of customers like Branson, McNerney is demonstrating that Boeing's efforts to reduce its environmental footprint will help it win new orders. And since Branson is so passionate about environmentalism—in 2007, he announced a $25 million prize for the first person to come up with a way to remove greenhouse gases from the atmosphere[16]—it may be that Virgin will be an early adopter of Boeing's cleaner products. Specifically, Branson anticipated that Boeing's 787 would help reduce the carbon footprint of Virgin's flights. As Branson said, "Virgin Atlantic is totally focused on delivering a cleaner airline in the air and on the ground, and our order today will significantly cut carbon emissions per flight."[17]

While many airlines are more concerned about surviving economically in an environment of rising fuel prices and a slowing economy, it is likely that more and more airlines will see the connection between a smaller environmental footprint and operating efficiency. And as more passengers shift their business to the more efficiently run airlines, Boeing's efforts to reduce its environmental footprint will appeal to other airlines like Virgin. As a result, Boeing will end up getting an even bigger payoff from its investment in more environmentally friendly products.

HE WORKS WITH GOVERNMENTS TO ENCOURAGE MORE STRINGENT ENVIRONMENTAL REGULATION

McNerney has also made it clear that he wants Boeing to take a leadership role in pushing the aircraft industry and global regulators to take action to reduce the aircraft industry's environmental impact. Why would an industry executive seek out *more* regulation rather than *less*? There are three reasons: First, McNerney believes that reducing the aircraft industry's environmental impact is the right thing to do. Second, he thinks such regulation will represent a business opportunity for Boeing because it will enjoy a competitive advantage in complying with those regulations and that will help Boeing win more business. Finally, McNerney believes that only through an industry-wide level playing field, which such regulation would create, can society receive the full benefit of reducing the airline industry's environmental impact. As McNerney puts it, "We also have to work with the industry. What we need to do is push for a global regulatory environment and global target setting for our industry. We're not quite there yet, but we want to participate. We want to play a stronger role than we've played before. It's the right issue. It isn't going away."[18]

But McNerney does not simply wish to cave in to the demands of different governments. Instead, he wants to encourage those governments to work together to create a mutually acceptable set of environmental standards. In so doing, McNerney hopes to help those governments achieve the appropriate balance between a cleaner environment and economic growth.

McNerney describes this effort, saying, "I think all governments, even in Europe, have to balance regulatory engineering to encourage more friendly products and behavior on one hand, and economic development on the other. That fundamental trade-off just doesn't go away. Even when you get to those countries in Europe where the rhetoric is the highest, the people that are promulgating the regulations are mindful of that trade-off. What I want to avoid is just mass confusion, where every country has a different carbon-trading scheme with different taxes. I really want to push for harmonization so our customers understand the envelope they are dealing with. We have to be part of that discussion. We can't just let that happen to us."[19]

Moreover, McNerney appears dedicated to understanding and responding to the economic incentives Boeing's customers, the airlines, are likely to face. In particular, McNerney wants Boeing to anticipate how governments will shape the tax system and the regulatory climate to encourage airlines to produce fewer pollutants and lower their noise levels. If Boeing can produce aircraft consistent with its customers' economic incentives, then customers will buy the aircraft and Boeing will benefit. As McNerney says, "We're not a government, but we do know that whatever happens it will encourage a lessening of the footprint of our products and lessening the impact of our production processes. We're going on that assumption. There will be economic incentives that our customers will face, and I want to make sure that it is a major part of the way we think about the products that we're going to develop."[20]

How does this help Boeing? Indirectly, Boeing will benefit because it is helping to shape the industry in a way that responds to the needs of the communities in which its customers operate. Specifically, if the airline industry is required to reduce its carbon emissions and to cut the noise it produces, then Boeing is likely to be the beneficiary. That's because Boeing's aircraft have smaller environmental footprints than those of Airbus. So the airlines, in seeking to comply with environmental regulation, will be better off if they choose Boeing aircraft. Simply put, Boeing's work to require consistent regulation of the airline industry's environmental footprint could yield higher revenues and profits for Boeing shareholders.

HE BOOSTS THE ROLE OF BOEING'S ENVIRONMENTAL STRATEGY DEPARTMENT

McNerney believes that Boeing's efforts to cut its environmental footprint are important. Yet with all his other responsibilities, he can only devote part of his time to those efforts. As a result, McNerney decided he needed help from a strong executive with the resources necessary to make a significant difference. To that end, McNerney boosted the role of Boeing's Environmental Strategy department, which had previously occupied a lower rung on Boeing's corporate ladder. McNerney made this organizational change in response to what he perceived as growing environmental concerns of its airline industry customers. As he said, "We've just reorganized our environmental team, raised it up in importance in the organization, put one of our big leaders in charge. The environment we want is always important for the customer, as they are the ones who have to face the brunt of protests."[21]

The big leader to whom McNerney referred was Bill Glover, BCA's director of environmental strategy. McNerney's idea was for Glover to spearhead a cultural change to make the environment a bigger concern throughout Boeing's operations. And he wanted Glover to accomplish this cultural change by setting specific targets for how Boeing would improve its environmental performance and how it would work with the aerospace industry to make big environmental improvements. Glover's promotion took place in December 2007 with the duty, as he put it, of building "a new organization, whose mission is to:

- Drive the environment issue into Boeing's very fabric
- Set aggressive targets for improving the environmental performance of Boeing's products, services and operations
- Help the aerospace industry advance."[22]

Moreover, Glover articulated a way that Boeing might achieve these lofty elements of the Environmental Strategy department's mission statement. Glover's strategy consists of four key elements: He wants Boeing to apply formal environmental standards, to measure its environmental footprint and reduce it systematically, to get all Boeing people involved in the effort, and to report to regulators and other communities on how well it's achieving these lofty goals. In Glover's words, "Our action plan comprises:

- **Alignment**—We are extending the International Standards Organization (ISO) 14001 universal standard certification for environmental management [a specific set of environmental management standards] from commercial airplanes facilities across our whole manufacturing operations.
- **Stewardship**—We are committed to continuously reducing our footprint by measuring it, setting targets and holding ourselves accountable.
- **Employee involvement**—We recognize that the skills and enthusiasm of Boeing's 150,000 employees are critical.
- **Heightened transparency and accountability**—to stakeholders and the world."[23]

One of Glover's key jobs in implementing this action plan is to change the way aircraft are routed from their departure points to their destinations, a process known as air traffic management (ATM). To that end, Boeing's Environmental Strategy unit is working with European governments to change ATM so that the airline industry will produce 12 percent lower CO_2 emissions. To achieve this ATM redesign, Boeing is working with airports, airlines, and civil aviation authorities at several international airports to make their operations more efficient, for example, by implementing the CDA procedures we discussed earlier. These CDA approach paths reduce public exposure to aircraft noise, lower aircraft fuel consumption, and diminish CO_2 emissions. Boeing believes that the investment required to achieve these benefits will help it reduce CO_2 to the target levels it has set for itself.[24]

Raising the importance of Boeing's Environmental Strategy department sends a signal to all of Boeing that McNerney cares about reducing the company's environmental footprint. But this organizational move also gives McNerney the extra help he needs to turn this lofty goal into the changed behavior Boeing needs to achieve his goals. If Glover fulfills McNerney's expectations, Boeing's customers and shareholders will be better off in the bargain.

McNerney's success reducing Boeing's environmental footprint illustrates four lessons for leaders:

- **Lead from the top.** McNerney decided to take a leadership role in cutting Boeing's environmental footprint. Why? To go beyond lip service, people throughout the company will need to act. And such action will only take place if the CEO expects it from the entire organization. In McNerney's case, he backed up the value he placed on environmental matters by promoting the Environmental Strategy unit and giving it the resources it needs to achieve its mission.

- **Know your constituents.** McNerney recognized that Boeing had an important and complex set of constituents for Boeing's environmental issues. In particular, he saw that the European government—with its desire to reduce chemical and noise pollution in its airports—could help Boeing's business if he responded to its concerns. He also recognized that if Boeing did not respond, then the European government could stunt its efforts there. Moreover, McNerney recognized that over time, the European emphasis on environmental matters would spread globally—to the United States and eventually to Asia. Therefore, paying attention to environmental concerns was more than good public relations, it was good business strategy.

- **Build momentum through quick wins.** As we saw in this chapter, Virgin Airlines' 787 order represented an important victory for Boeing over Airbus. And the key to that victory was Virgin's perception that the 787 was more environmentally friendly and likely to be available sooner than Airbus's competing A350 model. This win is an example of how a positive response can build internal momentum within a company for continuing to reduce its environmental footprint.

- **Extend scope to sustain benefits.** McNerney made it clear that Boeing would continue to work on ways to extend the benefits of cutting its environmental footprint. In Boeing's announcement with Virgin, for example, McNerney committed to experimenting with biofuels, which would also be expected to reduce CO_2 and NOX emissions. Moreover, Boeing was clearly investing R&D funds in new technologies, such as fuel cell batteries, and new ways of approaching airports.

CONCLUSION

McNerney's efforts to cut Boeing's environmental footprint have paid off for Boeing's shareholders. Its ability to knock competitor Airbus out of the running for an aircraft order from Virgin Airlines indicates that this principle has a tangible payoff. Moreover, the emphasis McNerney has placed on this principle—by elevating Boeing's Environmental Strategy unit, investing in R&D to reduce the environmental footprint of its products, working with Boeing's constituents to reduce its environmental footprint—attests to the business wisdom of cutting a company's environmental footprint.

ACKNOWLEDGMENTS

Industry experts, editors, and my family helped me write this book.

I am grateful to aircraft industry experts for their insights into Jim McNerney and the dynamics of the competition between Boeing and Airbus. These people include Richard Aboulafia, Philip Bolt, Wolfgang Demisch, George Hamlin, Doug McVitie, and Heidi Wood. I appreciate the insights of professors including U. Srinivasa Rangan at Babson College and Alan MacCormack at Harvard Business School. I want to thank those who offered their insights on condition of anonymity. Their comments helped shape my thinking and appeared throughout the book.

I also deeply appreciate the help of the Portfolio team. Jeffrey Krames, my editor, sought me out to write this book after reading my blog posts about the careers of Jack Welch's successors—which included Jim McNerney. Jeffrey made available a team of top-notch professionals—including Nancy Cardwell, whose brilliantly clear thinking helped me to focus this book on McNerney's lessons for leaders.

This book would not have been possible without the support of my family. My wife and children each helped in their own way—providing critiques of the manuscript and offering technical support. My parents helped in my efforts to pick a title for the book. And my brothers provided great moral support.

Chuck Roush, to whom this book is dedicated, has been a powerful example for me of what leadership is all about during the twenty-six years I've known him. A former air force officer who holds a doctorate in accounting from Harvard Business School, Chuck has taught me many things during my career. I am grateful for his help in thinking through what leadership means, and his own approach helped me recognize many of Jim McNerney's greatest leadership traits.

NOTES

INTRODUCTION: YOU CAN'T ORDER CHANGE

1. G. Norris, G. Thomas, M. Wagner, and C. Forbes Smith, *Boeing 787—Flying Redefined.* (Aerospace Technical Publications International, 2005).
2. Marilyn Adams, "Straightened Up and Flying Right," *USA Today,* February 26, 2007. Available at http://www.usatoday.com/money/companies/management/2007-02-25-exec-profile-boeing_x.htm.
3. Heidi Wood, interview with the author, March 7, 2008.
4. Ibid.
5. Peter Cohan, "Value Leadership: The Principles Driving Corporate Value," *Business Strategy Review,* Winter 2003, 31.
6. Del Jones, "Grading GE's Dream Team 5 Years Later," *USA Today,* September 7, 2006. Available at http://www.usatoday.com/money/companies/management/2006-09-07-ge-5years-later_x.htm.
7. Data for GE are from September 7, 2001, to June 9, 2008. Data for Boeing are from July 1, 2005, to June 9, 2008. Available at http://finance.google.com/finance?cid=626307.
8. Heidi Wood, interview with the author, March 7, 2008.
9. James McNerney, "2007 Address to Shareholders," April 30, 2007. Available at http://www.boeing.com/news/speeches/2007/mcnerney_070430.html.

10 Karen West, "How Boeing Transformed the Aviation Industry," MSNBC, July 2, 2007. Available at http://www.msnbc.msn.com/id/192421415/.

11. Renae Merle, "Boeing Agrees to Pay $615 Million Settlement," *Washington Post*, May 16, 2006, A10.

CHAPTER 1. HELP YOUR PEOPLE GET 15 PERCENT BETTER

1. Geoffrey Colvin, "How One CEO Learned to Fly," *Fortune*, October 16, 2006. Available at http://money.cnn.com/2006/10/16/magazines/fortune/Secrets_greatness_McNerney_Boeing.fortune/index.htm.

2. "Shared Corporate Values Key to Develop Leadership," *Nikkei Weekly*, December 13, 2004.

3. Boeing Corporate Values include: Leadership, Integrity, Quality, Customer Satisfaction, People Working Together, A Diverse and Involved Team, Good Corporate Citizenship, and Enhancing Shareholder Value. See http://www.boeing.com/companyoffices/aboutus/ethics/integst.htm.

4. James McNerney, "Address to Shareholders," May 1, 2006. Available at http://www.boeing.com/news/speeches/2006/mcnerney_060501.html.

5. Ameet Sachdev, "No Flights of Fancy," *Chicago Tribune*, June 24, 2006. Available at http://archive.seacoastonline.com/news/06242006/biz_nati/108833.htm.

6. McNerney, "Address to Shareholders."

7. A retired GE executive, interview with the author, February 29, 2008.

8. Ibid.

9. Ibid.

10. Colvin, "How One CEO Learned to Fly."

11. Michael Arndt, "Online Extra: The Hard Work in Leadership," *BusinessWeek*, April 12, 2004. Available at http://www.businessweek.com/magazine/content/04_15/b3878012_mz001.htm.

12. Ibid.

13. A retired GE executive, interview.

14. "Boeing Names Shanahan to Lead 787 Program, Bair to Lead Business Strategy and Marketing," Boeing.com, October 16, 2007. Available at http://www.boeing.com/news/releases/2007/q4/071016c_nr.html.

15. J. Lynn Lunsford, "Boeing CEO Fights Headwind," *Wall Street Journal*, April 25, 2008, B1.

16. Stanley Holmes, "Boeing: What Really Happened," *BusinessWeek*, December 15, 2003. Available at http://www.businessweek.com/magazine/content/03_50/b3862001_mz001.htm.

17. Heidi Wood, interview with the author, March 7, 2008.

18. Ibid.

19. Heidi Wood, interview with the author. June 11, 2008

20. Ibid.

21. John S. McLenahen, "New World Leader," *Industry Week*, January 1, 2004. Available at http://www.industryweek.com/PrintArticle.aspx?ArticleID=1368.

22. Ibid.

23. Arndt, "Online Extra."

24. James McNerney, "How We're Going to Improve Performance," Boeing.com, February 1, 2006. Available at http://www.boeing.com/news/speeches/2006/Mcnerney_060201.html.

25. Arndt, "Online Extra."

26. Doug McVitie, interview with the author, April 30, 2008.

27. Ibid.

28. Ibid.

CHAPTER 2. LEAD GROUPS TO HIGHER GROUND

1. Marilyn Adams, "Straightened Up and Flying Right," *USA Today*, February 26, 2007.

2. Dominic Gates, "Expectations Sky-High for New Boeing Leader," *Seattle Times*, July 1, 2005. Available at http//community.Seattletimes.nwsource.com/archive/?date=20050701&slug=mcnerney01.

3. Lisa Lerer, "The Year's Biggest Hires, Fires and Retires," *Forbes*, December 6, 2006. Available at http://www.forbes.com/2006/12/

06/leadership-managing-careers-lead-careers-cx_ll_1206hfr06
.html.

4. Heidi Wood, interview with the author, March 7, 2008.

5. Ibid.

6. Ibid.

7. Peter Robison and James Gunsalus, "Boeing Chief Tackles Ethics,
   All-New Jet," Bloomberg News, May 29, 2006. Available at http://
   seattlepi.nwsource.com/business/271937_boeingmcnerney29
   .html.

8. Ibid.

9. Ibid.

10. Ibid.

11. Gates, "Expectations Sky-High."

12. Ibid.

13. Ibid.

14. Robison and Gunsalus, "Boeing Chief Tackles Ethics."

15. Michael Arndt, "Online Extra: The Hard Work in Leadership,"
    BusinessWeek, April 12, 2004.

16. Robison and Gunsalus, "Boeing Chief Tackles Ethics."

17. A retired GE executive, interview with the author, February 29,
    2008.

18. Ibid.

CHAPTER 3. LINK PAY TO PROFIT AND PROCESS, NOT STOCK PRICE

1. Boeing Company, Boeing Definitive Proxy Statement, March 23,
   2007, 27. Available at http://www.sec.gov/Archives/edgar/data/12927/
   000119312507062748/ddef14a.htm.

2. Dominic Gates, "Expectations Sky-High for New Boeing Leader,"
   Seattle Times, July 1, 2005.

3. Ibid.

4. Ibid.

5. Carol Hymowitz, "Winning the Support of the Rank and File," *Ca-
   reerjournal.com*, April 24, 2002.

6. "Raising the Bar on Innovation," Coachingtip.blog, July 2005. Available at http://coachingtip.blogs.com/coaching_tip/2005/07/raising_the_bar.html.

7. Hymowitz, "Winning the Support."

8. Ibid.

9. Peter Robison and James Gunsalus, "Boeing Chief Tackles Ethics, All-New Jet," Bloomberg News, May 29, 2006.

10. Stanley Holmes, "Cleaning Up Boeing," *BusinessWeek*, March 13, 2006. Available at http://www.businessweek.com/magazine/content/06_11/b3975088.htm.

11. Boeing, Definitive Proxy Statement.

CHAPTER 4. BUILD STRATEGY ON CUSTOMER FOCUS

1. Peter Cohan, "The Technology Leaders: How America's Most Profitable High Tech Companies Innovate Their Way to Success" (San Francisco: Jossey-Bass Publishers, 1997), 14.

2. J. Lynn Lunsford, "Piloting Boeing's New Course," *Wall Street Journal*, June 13, 2006. Available at http://www.post-gazette.com/pg/06164/697889-28.stm#.

3. Andrea Trujillo Guajardo and Ross Partner, "Boeing CEO Offers UM Students Advice About Careers, Innovation," *Monroe Street Journal*, March 19, 2007. Available at http://www.themsj.com/home/index.cfm?event=displayArticlePrinterFriendly&uStory_id=58908f8b-ddcf-4e98-8eff-d761e5698606.

4. Ibid.

5. Ibid.

6. Lunsford, "Piloting Boeing's New Course."

7. Guajardo and Partner, "Boeing CEO Offers UM Students Advice."

8. A retired GE executive, interview with the author, February 29, 2008.

9. Heidi Wood, interview with the author, March 7, 2008.

10. Ibid.

11. Stanley W. Kandebo, "GE Wins Exclusive Deal to Power Long-Range 777s Boeing Selected the GE90 over Two Rivals Because 'It Best Met

the Overall Evaluation Criteria'," *Aviation Week & Space Technology*, July 12, 1999, 22.

12. Ibid.

13. Ibid.

14. Stanley Holmes, "Cleaning Up Boeing," *BusinessWeek*, March 13, 2006.

15. Guajardo and Partner, "Boeing CEO Offers UM Students Advice."

16. A retired GE executive, interview.

17. Mark Tatge, "Prescription for Growth," *Forbes*, February 17, 2003. Available at http://members.forbes.com/forbes/2003/0217/064_print .html.

18. Tim Stevens, "3M Reinvents Its Innovation Process," *Research-Technology Management*, March 1, 2004. Available at http://www .allbusiness.com/technology/762843-1.html.

19. Ibid.

20. Tatge, "Prescription for Growth."

21. Stevens, "3M Reinvents Its Innovation."

22. Ibid.

23. Tim Studt, "3M—Where Innovation Rules," *R&D*, April 1, 2003. Available at http://www.rdmag.com/ShowPR.aspx?PUBCODE=014 &ACCT=1400000100&ISSUE=0304&RELTYPE=PR&ORIGREL TYPE=FE&PRODCODE=00000000&PRODLETT=AH&Common Count=0.

24. James McNerney, "3M—Company View," *Datamonitor Company Profiles*, July 21, 2004.

CHAPTER 5. INVEST IN YOUR STRENGTHS

1. James Wallace, "Aerospace Notebook: Putting 'Lean' Processes into All of Boeing," *Seattle Post-Intelligencer*, January 11, 2006. Available at http://seattlepi.nwsource.com/business/255187_air11.html.

2. Peter Cohan, "When the Blind Lead," *Business Strategy Review*, Autumn 2007, 66.

3. Richard Aboulafia, interview with the author, May 20, 2008.

4. Richard Aboulafia, interview with the author, January 24, 2008.

5. Aboulafia, May 20, 2008, interview.

6. Srini Rangan, interview with the author, January 4, 2008. Rangan notes that the study, which took place between 1994 and 1996, delayed Airbus's investment in the A380 until the end of 1998. The result was that Boeing was able to extend its "monopoly rent [on the 747] four to five years."

7. Aboulafia, January 24, 2008, interview.

8. John Walsh, interview with the author, February 5, 2008.

9. Staff, "Only the Paranoid Survive: At First Anniversary, Boeing Chief Talks About the 787, Airbus and His Strategies for Managing 154,000 Employees," *Aviation Week & Space Technology*, June 26, 2006, 48.

10. Ibid.

11. Paul Nisbet, interview with the author, May 16, 2008.

12. Ibid.

13. Ibid.

14. Ibid.

15. Ibid.

16. Ibid.

17. Aboulafia, May 20, 2008, interview.

18. In October 2006, BEA Systems sold its 20 percent interest to EADS. "BAE Systems Says Completed Sale of Airbus Stake to EADS," *AFX News Limited*, October 13, 2006. Available at http://www.forbes.com/markets/feeds/afx/2006/10/13/afx3089453.html.

19. "The High Altitude War Between Boeing and Airbus," *Knowledge@Wharton*, June 28, 2006. Available at http://www.wharton.universia.net/index.cfm?fa=viewfeature&id=1186&language=english.

20. Ibid.

21. At the time, Airbus was a collection of nationally owned aerospace firms in the UK, Spain, Germany, and France. By 2002, EADS became their parent. Aboulafia, May 20, 2008, interview.

22. Phillip Bolt, interview with the author, February 15, 2008.

23. A European industry insider, interview with the author, February 20, 2008.

24. Aboulafia, May 20, 2008, interview.

25. "High Altitude War."

26. Nisbet, interview.

27. Angela Jameson, "Boeing Chief Bets That Being Biggest Is Not Best in Struggle for the Skies," *Times Online*, July 24, 2006. Available at http://www.timesonline.co.uk/tol/life_and_style/career_and_ jobs/senior_executive/article691726.ece.

28. Eight hundred ninety-six orders include 817 as of January 3, 2008, plus 79 orders through July 22, 2008. "Boeing Sets Third Consecutive Record for Commercial Airplane Orders in 2007," Boeing Web site, January 3, 2008. Available at http://www.Boeing.com/ news/releases/2008/91/080103d_nr.html and "Orders and Deliveries," Boeing Web site, July 29, 2008. Available at http://active .boeing.com/commercial/orders/index.cfm.

CHAPTER 6. GROW THROUGH PEOPLE, NOT DEALS

1. James Wallace, "Aerospace Notebook: Putting 'Lean' Processes into All of Boeing," *Seattle Post-Intelligencer*, January 11, 2006. Available at http://seattlepi.nwsource.com/business/255187_air11.html.

2. Emily Kearney, "McNerney Drives Organic Growth at 3M," *CTPID News*, February 18, 2005. Available at http://web.mit.edu/ctpid/ www/mcnerney.html.

3. Ibid.

4. Ibid.

5. Ibid.

6. John S. McClenahen, "New World Leader," *Industry Week,* January 1, 2004. Available at http://www.industryweek.com/ReadArticle .aspx?ArticleID=1368.

7. Kearney, "McNerney Drives Organic Growth."

8. Ibid.

9. J. Lynn Lunsford, "Piloting Boeing's New Course," *Wall Street Journal*, June 13, 2006. Available at http://www.post-gazette.com/ pg/06164/697889-28.stm#.

10. James McNerney, "2007 Address to Shareholders," April 30, 2007. Available at http://www.boeing.com/news/speeches/2007/mcnerney _070430.html.

11. Adrian Schofield, "Boeing Chooses Hill for New Development and Strategy Post," *Aviation Daily*, March 22, 2006, 3.

12. Marc Sklar, "Listen, Know, Adapt, Thrive," *Boeing Frontiers*, March 2006. Available at http://www.boeing.com/news/frontiers/archive/2006/march/i_ids1.html.

13. McClenahen, "New World Leader."

14. Ibid.

15. 3M Company, 2003 Form 10-K, March 10, 2004. Available at http://www.sec.gov/Archives/edgar/data/66740/000089710104000425/mmm041053s1_10k.htm.

16. McClenahen, "New World Leader."

17. "3M Co Looks to Emerging Markets for Continued Growth," 3M Touch Systems, February 21, 2005. Available at http://www.industrysearch.co.uk/News/3M_Co_looks_to_emerging_markets_for_continued_growth-16127.

18. Ibid.

19. Ibid.

20. Mark Haines and Joe Kernen, "3M—CHMN & CEO—Interview," *CNBC/Dow Jones Business Video*, December 20, 2002.

21. 3M Co., 2003 Form 10-K.

22. TeleTrader News Room, "3M Reorganizes Businesses, Reshuffles Executives," *VLBG News*, September 27, 2002.

23. 3M Co., 2003 Form 10-K.

24. TeleTrader News Room, "3M Reorganizes Businesses."

25. "3M CEO: Customer Dedication, Innovation Driving Solid Growth Momentum; Shareholders Elect Directors, Ratify Appointment of Auditors and Approve Increase in Authorized Shares," *Business Wire*, May 11, 2004. Available at http://findarticles.com/p/articles/mi_m0EIN/is_2004_May_11/ai_n6021431/print.

26. James McNerney, "2008 Address to Shareholders," April 28, 2008. Available at http://www.boeing.com/news/speeches/2008/mcnerney_080428.html.

27. Ibid.

28. Ibid.

29. Ibid.

30. Ibid.

31. Ibid.

32. Ibid.

33. 3M Co., Form 2003 10-K.

34. Haines and Kernen, "3M—CHMN & CEO—Interview."

35. "3M to Acquire Corning Precision Lens; Technology Will Accelerate 3M's Growth," *Business Wire*, November 12, 2002. Available at http://findarticles.com/p/articles/mi_m0EIN/is_2002_Nov_12/ai_94155397/print.

36. Ibid.

37. Don Baker, "3M Purchasing Clormont Lens Firm for $850M," *Cincinnati Post*, November 12, 2002, A1.0.

38. Haines and Kernen, "3M—CHMN & CEO—Interview."

39. James McNerney, "2007 Address to Shareholders," April 30, 2007. Available at http://www.boeing.com/news/speeches/2007/mcnerney_070430.html.

40. Francine Knowles, "Boeing Paying $1.7 Bil. for Air Service Giant Aviall," *Chicago Sun-Times*, May 2, 2006, 49.

41. Ibid.

42. James McNerney, "Turbocharging Boeing," *Flight International*, June 27, 2006, 16–17.

CHAPTER 7. TACKLE CHALLENGING SITUATIONS QUICKLY AND EFFECTIVELY

1. Robert Weisman, "With Economy's Growth, CEOs Are in High Demand," *Boston Globe*, July 22, 2007. Available at http://www.boston.com/business/articles/2007/07/22/with_economys_growth_ceos_are_in_high_demand/.

2. Peter Robison and James Gunsalus, "Boeing Chief Tackles Ethics, All-New Jet," *Bloomberg News*, May 29, 2006.

3. A retired GE executive, interview with the author, May 30, 2008.

4. Ibid.

5. Ibid.

6. Ibid.

7. Ibid.

8. Michael Arndt, "3M's Rising Star," *BusinessWeek*, April 12, 2004.

Available at http://www.businessweek.com/magazine/content/04_15/
63878001_mz001.htm.

9. Ibid.

10. Ibid.

11. Ibid.

12. A retired GE executive, interview.

13. Dianne Brady, " 'Being Mean Is So Last Millennium'," *Business-Week,* January 4, 2007. Available at http://www.businessweek.com/
print/bwdaily/dnflash/content/jan2007/db20070103_618602.htm.

14. A retired GE executive, interview.

15. Ibid.

16. Ibid.

17. Ibid.

18. Ann Keeton, "Boeing CEO: Commercial Airplane Backlog Could Grow in '06" Dow Jones News Service, February 7, 2006.

19. Dave Carpenter, "Boeing CEO Oversees Smooth Sailing, Targets Ethics in First Year," Associated Press, June 30, 2006.

20. Ibid.

21. Dominic Gates, "Booming Boeing Aims Even Higher," *Seattle Times,* February 2, 2006. Available at http://seattletimes.nwsource.
com/html/businesstechnology/2002777474_boeing02.html.

22. A retired GE executive, interview.

23. James McNerney, "Learning to Lead," Boeing Web site, November 1, 2007. Available at http://www.boeing.com/news/speeches/2007/
mcnerney_071106.html.

24. Ibid.

25. Ibid.

26. Ibid.

CHAPTER 8. TIGHTEN OPERATIONS WITH PROCESS-IMPROVEMENT TOOLS

1. John S. McClenahen, "New World Leader," *Industry Week,* January 1, 2004.

2. James P. Womack, Daniel T. Jones, and Daniel Roos, *The Machine That Changed the World* (New York: HarperPerennial, 1991), 49.

3. Kevin Maler, "3M Adopts Quality Control Program to Boost Performance," *Knight Ridder Tribune Business News—KRTBN*, April 4, 2001.

4. Reg Birchfield, "The Management Interview: Laurie Altman: Abrasive Background," *Management*, August 1, 2003, 32.

5. Ibid.

6. Claudia H. Deutsch, "In a Cost-Cutting Move, 3M Says It Will Eliminate 5,000 Jobs," *New York Times*, April 24, 2001. Available at http://query.nytimes.com/gst/fullpage.html?res=9A0DEED 81F30F937A15757C0A9679C8B63&sec=&spon=&pagewanted= print.

7. Ibid.

8. McClenahen, "New World Leader."

9. Ibid.

10. James McNerney, "2007 Address to Shareholders," April 30, 2007. Available at http://www.boeing.com/news/speeches/2007/mcnerney _070430.html.

11. Taichi Ohno, "Toyota Production System," Productivity Press, March 1, 1988, 8.

12. Katherine Beck and Carrie Thearle, "Out of the Office, Onto the Shop Floor," *Boeing Frontiers*, August 2006. Available at http:// www.boeing.com/news/frontiers/archive/2006/august/cover.pdf.

13. "787 Program Update Conference Call—Final," Vocant Fair Disclosure Wire, December 11, 2007.

14. A retired GE executive, interview with the author, May 30, 2008.

15. "787 Program Update Conference Call."

16. Boeing is anticipated to deliver only twenty-five 787s in 2009. James Wallace, "James Wallace on Aerospace," *Seattle-Post Intelligencer*, May 8, 2008. Available at http://blog.seattlepi.nwsource.com/aero- space/archives/138480.asp.

17. "787 Program Update Conference Call."

18. Ibid.

19. Ibid.

20. Doug Cameron, "Text of Jim McNerney Interview," *FT.com*, June 10, 2007, http://www.ft.com/cms/s/0/f3c10574-15fb-11dc-a7ce-000b5 df10621.html.

21. "Time to Learn, Share" *Boeing Frontiers,* June 2007. Available at http://www.boeing.com/news/frontiers/archive/2007/june/qt_ab.pdf.
22. Ibid.
23. Ibid.
24. Beck and Thearle, "Out of the Office."
25. Ibid.
26. Ibid.
27. Ibid.
28. Ibid.
29. Ibid.
30. Ibid.
31. Cameron, "Text of Jim McNerney Interview."
32. "787 Program Update Conference Call."
33. Ibid.
34. Ibid.
35. A retired GE executive, interview.
36. Ibid.
37. Ibid.

CHAPTER 9: PARTNER WITH GLOBAL SUPPLIERS TO REDUCE RISK AND ACCELERATE TIME TO MARKET

1. Maria Bartiromo, "Facetime with Boeing's Jim McNerney," *BusinessWeek,* May 28, 2008. Available at http://www.businessweek.com/print/magazine/content/08_23/b4087000734432.htm.
2. John Dodge, "Boeing 787 Dreamliner Engineering Chief Describes Partners," *Design News,* May 15, 2007. Available at http://www.designnews.com/index.asp?layout=articlePrint&articleID=CA6441528.
3. A retired GE executive, interview with the author, May 30, 2008.
4. Karen West, "Dreamliner Delay Is Wake-up Call for Boeing," MSNBC, October 11, 2007. Available at http://www.msnbc.msn.com/id/21250495/.
5. David Greising and Michael Oneal, "The Global Factor," *Chicago Tribune,* February 23, 2005. Available at www.chicagotribune.com/news/specials/chi-0502230190feb23,0,7081112.story.

6. Ibid.

7. Ibid.

8. Ibid.

9. Ibid.

10. Ibid.

11. Alan MacCormack, Harvard Business School associate professor, interview with the author, April 11, 2008.

12. Heidi Wood, interview with the author, March 7, 2008.

13. Ibid.

14. Ibid.

15. A retired GE executive, interview.

16. Ibid.

17. Ibid.

18. George Hamlin, interview with the author, February 5, 2008.

19. Ibid.

20. Ibid.

21. Ibid.

22. European industry insider, interview with the author, February 20, 2008.

23. Wolfgang Demisch, interview with the author, February 25, 2008.

24. Ibid.

25. A retired GE executive, interview.

26. Sean Snyder, "Boeing Delays Production First Flight of 787 Dreamliner," *Design News*, January 16, 2008. Available at http://www.designnews.com/article/CA6523105.html.

27. A retired GE executive, interview.

28. J. Lynn Lunsford, "Boeing CEO Fights Headwind," *Wall Street Journal*, April 25, 2008, B1.

29. John Dodge, "Boeing 787 Delay Nets First Casualty, Mike Bair," *Design News*, October 17, 2007. Available at http://www.designnews.com/article/CA6492177.html.

30. James Wallace, "Boeing 787 Gives Investors a Sudden Fright," *Seattle Post-Intelligencer*, October 26, 2006. Available at http://seattlepi.nwsource.com/business/290032_boeingearns26.html.

31. Ibid.

32. J. Lynn Lunsford, "Boeing Scrambles to Repair Problems with New Plane," *Wall Street Journal,* December 7, 2007, A1.

33. Ibid.

34. Lunsford, "Boeing CEO Fights Headwind."

35. P-I News Services, "Boeing Continues Damage Control on Two Fronts," seattlepi.com, March 28, 2008, http://seattlepi.nwsource .com/business/356953_boeingvought29.html.

36. James Wallace, "Boeing Sticks to Global Plan," *Seattle Post-Intelligencer,* May 5, 2008. Available at http://seattlepi.nwsource .com/business/361880_boeing06.html?source=rss.

37. Michael Mecham, "Contrite Boeing Announces Third Delay in 787 Program," *Aviation Week,* January 20, 2008. Available at http:// www.aviationweek.com/aw/generic/story_generic.jsp?channel=awst &id=news/aw012108p3.xml.

38. Bartiromo, "Facetime with Boeing's Jim McNerney."

CHAPTER 10. MAKE ETHICS AND COMPLIANCE A CLEAR COMPETITIVE ADVANTAGE

1. Dominic Gates and Alicia Mundy, "Boeing Lawyer Warns of Company's Legal Peril," *Seattle Times,* January 31, 2006. Available at http://seattletimes.nwsource.com/cgi-bin/PrintStory.pl?document_ id=2002772936&zsection_id=2002119995&slug=boeing31&date= 20060131.

2. Leslie Wayne, "Senate Critic Now Praises Boeing Chief," *New York Times,* August 2, 2006, http://www/nytimes.com/2006/08/02/ business/02boeing.html.

3. Marilyn Adams, "Straightened Up and Flying Right," *USA Today,* February 26, 2007.

4. A retired GE executive, interview with the author, May 30, 2008.

5. Ibid.

6. Ibid.

7. James McNerney, "Turning Ethics and Compliance into a Competitive Advantage," April 27, 2006. Available at http://www.boeing .com/news/speeches/2006/mcnerney_060427.html.

8. Ibid.

9. Gates and Mundy, "Boeing Lawyer Warns of Company's Legal Peril."

10. Ibid.

11. Ibid.

12. Ibid.

13. Stanley Holmes, "Cleaning Up Boeing," *BusinessWeek*, March 3, 2006. Available at http://www.businessweek.com/magazine/content/06_11/b3975088.htm.

14. Gates and Mundy, "Boeing Lawyer Warns of Company's Legal Peril."

15. Ibid.

16. Ibid.

17. Holmes, "Cleaning Up Boeing."

18. James McNerney, "Ethics and Compliance 'Are All About the Future'," *Boeing Frontiers*, December 2005. Available at http://www.boeing.com/news/frontiers/archive/2005/december/i_lm.html.

19. Roseanne Gerin, "Boeing CEO Calls Settlement 'Tough But Fair'," *Washington Technology*, August 2, 2006. Available at http://www.washingtontechnology.com/cgi-bin/udt/im.display.printable?client.id=washingtontechnology_daily&story.id=29050.

20. Associated Press, "Boeing CEO Sees Smooth Sailing in 1st Year," July 2, 2006. Available at http://tamil.sify.com/news/fullstory.php?id=1424025.

21. Stanley Holmes, "Boeing Does the 'Right Thing'," *BusinessWeek*, July 27, 2006. Available at http://www.businessweek.com/investor/content/jul2006/pi20060727_170256.htm?chan=top ews_top+news.

22. A retired GE executive, interview.

23. Holmes, "Boeing Does the 'Right Thing.'"

24. James McNerney, "Statement of W. James McNerney, Jr., Chairman, President & CEO, The Boeing Company, Before the U.S. Senate Committee on Armed Services, Tuesday, August 1, 2006." Available at http://www.globalsecurity.org/military/library/congress/2006_hr/060801-mcnerney.pdf.

25. Ibid.

26. Ibid.

27. Ibid.

28. Ibid.

29. McNerney, "Ethics and Compliance 'Are All About the Future.'"

30. Seek out performance reviews of an individual from all those who interact with the employee—including his or her subordinates, peers, and boss.

31. Holmes, "Cleaning Up Boeing."

32. McNerney, "Turning Ethics and Compliance into a Competitive Advantage."

33. Ibid.

34. McNerney, "Statement Before the U.S. Senate Committee on Armed Services."

CHAPTER 11. CUT YOUR COMPANY'S ENVIRONMENTAL FOOTPRINT

1. "Airlines Turn to Plastics to Reduce Carbon Footprint," *Earthnews*, June 18, 2007. Available at http://www.earthportal.org/news/?p=216.

2. Doug Cameron, "Text of Jim McNerney Interview," *FT.com*, June 10, 2007, http://www.ft.com/cms/s/0/f3c10574-15fb-11dc-a7ce-000b5 df10 621.html.

3. Ibid.

4. Ibid.

5. Ibid.

6. Ibid.

7. Ibid.

8. Symposium Abstracts, "Air Transportation: The Environmental Challenge," December 6, 2007.

9. Ibid.

10. Ibid.

11. Ibid.

12. Ibid.

13. Ashley M. Heher, "Big 787 Orders Come Flying In," Associated Press, April 25, 2007. Available at http://seattletimes.nwsource.com/html/businesstechnology/2003680175_boeingorders25.html.

14. Michael Harrison, "Virgin Atlantic Gives $8bn Order to Boeing in

Fresh Setback for Airbus," *Independent*, April 25, 2007. Available at
http://www.independent.co.uk/news/business/news/virgin-atlantic
-gives-8bn-order-to-boeing-in-fresh-setback-for-airbus-446136
.html

15. Ibid.

16. Tariq Panja, "British Tycoon Branson Offers $25 Million Prize to
Fight Climate Change," Associated Press, February 9, 2007. Available at http://www.usatoday.com/tech/science/2007-02-09-branson
-climate-prize_x.htm.

17. James Wallace, "Aerospace Notebook: Efficient 787 Wins Over Virgin Atlantic," *Seattle Post-Intelligencer*, April 25, 2007. Available at
http://seattlepi.nwsource.com/business/312955_air25.html.

18. Cameron, "Text of Jim McNerney Interview."

19. Ibid.

20. Ibid.

21. Ibid.

22. Symposium Abstracts, "Air Transportation."

23. Ibid.

24. Ibid.

INDEX